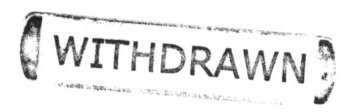

Vignettes from the Late Ming

Vignettes from the Late Ming

A *Hsiao-p'in* Anthology

Translated
with
Annotations
and an
Introduction
by
YANG YE

University of Washington Press

SEATTLE AND LONDON

Library of Congress Cataloging-in-Publication Data
Vignettes from the late Ming : a hsiao-p'in anthology / translated with
annotations and an introduction by Yang Ye.
    p. cm.
Includes bibliographical references and index.
ISBN 0–295–97733–7 (alk. paper)
    1. Chinese essays—Ming dynasty, 1368–1644—Translations into
English. I. Ye, Yang, 1948– .
PL2658.E8V54   1999   98–15078
895.1'44608—dc21   CIP

For Cora, Joy, and Sean

Contents

Acknowledgments

The project that has crystallized into this present volume took its first step in 1991, when I received a Summer Stipend from the National Endowment for the Humanities (NEH) for a study of the T'ung-ch'eng school, which dominated the Chinese literary stage from the mid-eighteenth century through the end of the Ch'ing dynasty. In my study I traced the canon back to the Ming author Kuei Yu-kuang, widely considered a predecessor, and I found that while Kuei certainly exerted a great influence on the Ch'ing writers, he was just as much (if not even more so) a man of his own age, an age that saw the rise of the *hsiao-p'in*, which in many ways is opposed to T'ung-ch'eng prose in its underlying principles. This led me to explore collections of Ming authors and eventually to complete this book.

Summer Research Support Awards, Academic Senate Travel Grants, and Intramural Research Funds from the University of California, Riverside, enabled me to search for and work on primary texts in the East Asian collections of UC Berkeley, UCLA, and Stanford, and to make a sentimental journey back to Harvard's Widener and Yenching libraries, where I received much help from my friend Daisy Chia-yaung Hu.

The chapter on Kuei Yu-kuang contains material I presented at the 1990 annual meeting of the New England Conference of the Association for Asian Studies (AAS) at Smith College, in a panel chaired by Susan Cherniack, a fellow devotee of Tu Fu. The chapter on Chang Tai contains material I presented at the October 1993 Joint Meeting of the International Studies Association, West Region (ISA-West), and Asian Studies on the Pacific Coast (ASPAC) at the Monterey Institute of International Studies. I would like to thank those in both audiences who raised interesting questions and helped me to sharpen my thoughts on related issues.

I am very much indebted to Irving Yucheng Lo, professor emeritus of Indiana University and an old family friend, who read the entire manuscript in the summer of 1995, checking my translation against the originals piece by piece, and sent me a detailed commentary, which helped me to make a thorough revision before I submitted the manuscript to publishers. A tribute is due to my former mentors at Harvard who read the manuscript: Stephen Owen, who first urged me to engage myself in studies of classical Chinese belles-lettres prose; and Patrick D. Hanan for his kind encouragement. I owe an intellectual debt to all previous works on the topic as listed in the Bibliography, but in particular to those of Jonathan Chaves and Chih-p'ing Chou.

I want to thank the two referees for the University of Washington Press for their valuable suggestions. I am honored to receive a nod of assent to the manuscript from Jonathan Chaves, who chose to reveal his identity, and I want to give him another salute here for his pioneering work on the Yüan brothers and his elegant translation, which serves as a model for emulation for me. I am very much obliged to David R. Knechtges, who had remained anonymous until he generously granted permission to use his comments on the jacket, for his staunch support and constructive criticism. To me he has always exemplified the very best of literary and philological scholarship, East or West. At the University of Washington Press, Lorri Hagman's graceful and meticulous editing, as well as Pamela Chaus's ingenious design of the text, helped to make this a much better book.

Standing out in what Oscar Wilde called "the diary that we all carry about with us," that is, memory, are days of my childhood and youth spent with my father, Ye Congqi, who home-schooled me in studies of Chinese classics, and with my eldest brother, Ye Zhi (better known by his pen name Zhu Wan as one of China's leading translators of Western literature), who taught me most of my English and introduced me to the beauty and diversity of the English essay from Addison and Steele to Max Beerbohm and G. K. Chesterton. My wife, Cora, has kept me afloat throughout my labor of love. I dedicate this book to her, and also to my children, Joy and Sean, who I hope will learn to enjoy the colors, sounds, and tastes in the world around us as much as did our late-Ming ancestors.

YY

Hsiao-p'in of the Late Ming
An Introduction

Periodization and Dominant Forms

The history of Chinese literature and arts has been perennially concerned with the issue of periodization. For each imperial dynasty, an art or literary form has been identified as representing its acme of creative power. Thus the ancient Shang dynasty is remembered for its splendid bronze art; the bombastic and elaborate rhapsody (*fu*) has been identified with the Western Han; and Chinese literary historians have always taken pride in discussing the superior accomplishments of the *shih* poetry of the T'ang, the song lyrics (*tz'u*) of the Sung, the *ch'ü*—which includes both "northern drama" (*tsa-chü*) and "individual arias" (*san-chü*)—of the Yüan, and the vernacular fiction of the Ming and the Ch'ing dynasties. Sometimes such periodization has been carried further to link one art or literary form with a particular period of imperial reign within a dynasty. Not unlike the ways the English have talked about their "Elizabethan poetry," "Restoration drama," "Queen Anne architecture," and "Victorian fiction," the Chinese have identified, for example, the kind of sensual poetry (*yen shih*) about love and women with the short-lived dynasties of the Ch'i (479–502) and the Liang (502–57), so that thenceforth such poems have frequently been called "poetry in the Ch'i-Liang style." The exquisite bronze incense burners and elegant porcelain vessels produced during Emperor Hsüan-tsung's Hsüan-te reign (1426–35) and the colorful cloisonné blue-glazed enamelware made during Emperor Tai-tsung's Ching-t'ai reign (1450–57), both of the Ming dynasty, have since been respectively called "Hsüan-te censers," "Hsüan-te porcelain," and "Ching-t'ai blue." Emperor Kao-tsung's Ch'ien-lung reign (1736–95) and Emperor Jen-tsung's Chia-ch'ing reign (1796–1820), both during the Ch'ing dynasty, have always been characterized by the extensive and thorough philological scholarship practiced by leading men of letters of that period, known later as "Ch'ien-Chia scholarship."

A concept introduced by the Russian Formalist critics may help us to better understand this cultural phenomenon. Culture may be understood as a system that consists of various interacting elements. In such a system, some elements are frequently projected into the foreground and become dominant, while others recede into the background. Roman Jacobson has defined the dominant as the foregrounding of one or a group of elements. In cultural history, the term has been used to refer to different genres of art—visual, musical, or verbal—which became dominant at various stages during the development of Western civilization. According to Jacobson, the dominant does not remain the same, but shifts from age to age. This shifting underscores the tension between canon and artistic novelty—the latter being understood as a deviation that often evolves into a new canon.[1]

We may use the concept of the dominant as a lens to examine, for example, the development of Chinese poetry. The rise of new poetic forms—such as regulated verse (*lü-shih*) in the seventh century, song lyrics in the tenth, and individual arias in the thirteenth—has indeed revealed a tension between the status quo and the pursuit for originality. Dissatisfied with following the prescribed order of their predecessors, some "strong poets" (to use Harold Bloom's term) experimented with new forms to find the best vehicle for their need for expression. At the hands of great masters, the new form flourished and gradually evolved into a new canon, until in due course it wore out and was superseded by another new form.

The *hsiao-p'in*, a short belles-lettres prose piece or vignette, usually informal in structure and mostly casual and spontaneous in mood and tone, was established as a literary genre during the last quarter of the sixteenth century. It became a dominant literary form of the late Ming period and flourished for nearly a century, until decades after the demise of the Ming. The *hsiao-p'in* has always been identified with the late Ming.[2]

Prototypical Forms and Spiritual Forefathers

Dominant as the *hsiao-p'in* was in the late Ming, it did not make its appearance on the Chinese literary stage like a thunderbolt from the sky. Compared with that in other civilizations, nonfictional prose enjoyed an honorable, long, and rich history in the Chinese tradition. Of the six ancient classics canonized during the Han dynasty as Confucian scriptures (*Ju ching*), four were in the form of prose. Prose flourished during the age of

"Contention of a Hundred Schools" (4th–3rd cent. B.C.E.) in the sayings and speeches of Chuang-tzu, Mencius, Han-fei-tzu, and the other thinkers. For the lengthy period before drama and fiction emerged on the literary horizon, nonfictional prose (*wen*) was considered to be the highest literary achievement, along with *shih* poetry.

Prototypes of the *hsiao-p'in* may be found in earlier literature. Ch'ien Mu (1895–1990), a leading modern scholar, argued that the form might be traced as far back as *The Analects* (Lun-yü) of Confucius, the book of *Chuang-tzu*, the "T'an Kung" chapter in *The Book of Rites* (Li-chi), and *Intrigues of the Warring States* (Chan-kuo ts'e)—all pre-Ch'in (before the early 2nd cent. B.C.E.) classics, generally considered to be works with serious moral and ethical significance.[3] The passages that Ch'ien Mu cited as examples of early *hsiao-p'in* are usually short descriptive sketches, such as this autobiographical profile from *The Analects*: "The Master said: 'I eat simple food and drink plain water. I lie down and support my head with my elbows. Happiness lies within all this. To enjoy wealth and rank without holding any higher principles—to me that is like a floating cloud'" (VII, 14).

Brief and simple as it is, this snapshot of a self-portrait of the Master preceded the autobiographical *hsiao-p'in* of the Ming authors. The passage from *The Analects* that is closest in spirit to the late Ming vignette is, in my opinion, the record of a conversation between Confucius and his disciples, which started like most of the more serious catechisms in the book: the Master asked his disciples to tell him about their ideals, and one by one they talked about their political ambitions. However, the dialogue unexpectedly changed tone when the Master called upon Tseng Tien, who had been playing on a zither (*se*) while the others were talking. He put the zither aside, sat up straight, and said, "Mine is different from those of the others." The Master said, "What's the harm? They were merely expressing what's on their mind—that's all." Feeling encouraged, Tseng Tien opened his mind: "In late spring, when our spring clothes are ready, in a group of five or six young men, and six or seven boys, we shall take a bath in the I River, stay in the breeze at the terrace [where ceremonies to worship Heaven are held], and return home singing all the way." The Master said, sighing, "I am with Tien" (XI, 24).

Orthodox Neo-Confucian philosophers of the Sung dynasty made laborious but largely irrelevant efforts to explain the Master's response, not realizing that it is exactly such passages in *The Analects* that best illustrate the amiable and unassuming personality of the sage. The sense of harmony with Nature, reflected in the Master's appreciation of Tseng Tien's spontaneous reply, exemplifies the inherently humanistic nature of Confucian teaching. This humanism was vividly expressed in the *hsiao-p'in*.

During the Six Dynasties,[4] literature became distinct from history, philosophy, and so on, and moved into a period of self-consciousness. Literati, who had moved with the Eastern Chin regime to the scenic Chiang-nan area, seem to have for the first time discovered an empathy with Nature and an appreciation of its beauty. During this period short prose pieces (including familiar letters, travel notes, and short life-sketches) were widely written and read. Indeed, in content many of these compositions are hardly distinguishable from late Ming *hsiao-p'in* pieces. Among the earliest examples of such compositions are, for example, a famous preface to a collection of poems written at a drinking party in celebration of the Bathing Festival at Orchid Pavilion (the occasion itself echoes Tseng Tien's "ideal" as recounted in *The Analects*), written by the "Sage of Calligraphy," Wang Hsi-chih (303?–61?).[5] Passages from *A Commentary on the Water Classic* (Shui-ching chu)[6] by Li Tao-yüan (d. 527) became the model of travel writing for later writers, from the T'ang master Liu Tsung-yüan (773–819) to late Ming *hsiao-p'in* writers such as Yüan Hung-tao* and Wang Ssu-jen.* *A New Account of Tales of the World* (Shih-shuo hsin-yü), a fifth-century collection of laconic but vividly drawn descriptions of the sayings and mannerisms of the statesmen, courtiers, and literati of the Wei and Chin dynasties, exerted a major influence on most of late Ming *hsiao-p'in* writers.[7] Wang Ssu-jen, with an idiosyncratic sense of humor, compared the passages in the book to "delicate appetizers" that could be taken daily to keep one from getting bored with the heavy "pork roast" of classics, such as Ssu-ma Ch'ien's (b. 145 or 135 B.C.E.) *Historical Records* (Shih-chi) and Pan Ku's (32–92) *History of the Han* (Han-shu).[8]

The late Ming authors of *hsiao-p'in* found another spiritual forefather in the versatile Sung writer Su Shih (or Su Tung-po, 1037–1101), whose *Memorabilia* (Chih-lin), a collection of short sketches, diaries, and miscellaneous random notes, was repeatedly reprinted, widely read, and regarded as a model for prose writing in the late sixteenth century. The following is a frequently anthologized piece from that book, often cited as a precursor text of the late Ming *hsiao-p'in*:

A Night Jaunt to Ch'eng-t'ien
It was the twelfth day of the tenth month in the sixth year of the Yüan-

* Asterisks indicate authors and *hsiao-p'in* pieces included in this anthology.

feng reign [1083]. At night I had already undressed and was about to go to bed, when the moonlight entered my room. Delighted, I got up and walked around. Then it hit upon me that I had no company to have fun with, so I went over to Ch'eng-t'ien Temple to call upon Chang Huai-ming. Huai-ming was not asleep either, so the two of us walked side by side in the middle of the courtyard. The courtyard, in an open sheet of light, looked like a pool with waterweed crisscrossing in it—which was actually the shadow of bamboos and cypress trees. Isn't the moon up there every night? Bamboos and cypresses—are they not to be found anywhere? What was unusual were just idle fellows like the two of us. (1981, p. 2; 1983, p. 4)[9]

This short piece was written by Su Shih three years after he had moved in his exile to Huang-chou, a remote prefecture in Hupei along the upper reaches of the Yangtze. Unlike the two famous "Rhapsodies on the Red Cliff" he wrote a year earlier, which are longer and more elaborate, this note excels in simplicity and spontaneity—exactly the qualities that characterize most late Ming *hsiao-p'in* compositions. Su Shih's prose writings were extremely popular during the late Ming period. The extant records of the hundreds of editions of his works, printed in the sixteenth and seventeenth centuries, are evidence that the Sung author definitely stayed a long time on the best-seller list during that period. Ch'en Wan-i, a leading scholar of the *hsiao-p'in* in Taiwan, enumerated some fifteen important editions of selections of Su Shih's prose printed between 1556 and 1644 (1988, pp. 7–10). Two of these were actually entitled *The Hsiao-p'in of Su Chang-kung*, and many included his shorter prose pieces from *Memorabilia*. Most major late Ming *hsiao-p'in* authors were enthusiastic about Su Shih's writing. Although this was partially due to the emulation of the Eight Prose Masters of the T'ang and Sung (including Su Shih) by sixteenth-century writers of the so-called T'ang-Sung school, what writers from Yüan Hung-tao to Chang Tai* particularly liked was Su Shih's shorter and less formal writings. Yüan Chung-tao* even observed that without his *hsiao-p'in* pieces, Su Shih would be "far less lovable."[10]

Despite these precursor texts, however, the *hsiao-p'in* was not established as an independent literary genre until the late sixteenth century, and it came to its peak only during the late Ming period, when new boundaries were reached, new possibilities were explored, and, last but not least, its own nomenclature was widely accepted.

The Rise of the *Hsiao-p'in* in the Late Ming

The term *hsiao-p'in* (lit., "small version" or "lesser type") has been traced to the beginning of the fifth century, when the Buddhist missionary Kumā-rajīva (344–413) was invited to settle down in the city of Ch'ang-an by Yao Hsing (366–416), ruler of the northern regime of the Later Ch'in. With the help of his Chinese disciples, Kumārajīva translated many Buddhist sutras into Chinese. He made two versions of the *Prajñāpāramitā Sūtra*, a collection of Mahayana Buddhist teachings—a longer one in twenty-seven sections (*chüan*),[11] the *Ta-p'in Prajñā* (Prajñā: The large version); and an abridged one in ten sections, the *Hsiao-p'in Prajñā* (Prajñā: The small version).[12] A little later in the century, the term *hsiao-p'in* was also found in *A New Account of Tales of the World*; its several appearances all referred to Kumārajīva's *Hsiao-p'in Prajñā*.[13] Obviously, the usage of the term was initiated primarily out of a practical categorizing need, and had nothing to do with literary genre.

Late Ming writers probably rediscovered the term from their enthusiastic reading of *A New Account of Tales of the World* and also out of a similar need to categorize prose—to distinguish the new form from longer and more formal writings, especially those modeled after Western Han prose as promoted by the neoclassicists who had dominated the literary stage. For centuries nonfictional prose had been regarded as "a vehicle for the Tao"— a literary means with a serious purpose. But late Ming authors, in their pursuit of novelty, found in the *hsiao-p'in* form a way to break away from ideological bondage and thus endowed the term with new meaning. The term came to refer specifically to short, informal belles-lettres prose that primarily served to amuse and entertain its reader. A number of writers of the period used the term in the titling collections of their own such writings, and a number of anthologies of such prose pieces by various authors, bearing the term in the title, are known to have been published in the late Ming period.[14] Ch'en Chi-ju,* a *hsiao-p'in* master himself, remarked on the rise of the new genre in the preface he wrote for an anthology of *hsiao-p'in* compiled by his friend Cheng Ch'ao-tsung, which was titled *Literary Amusement* (Wen yü):

> In the past, before the year of 1627, the eunuch's network of informers spread all around. I told Lord Tung [Ch'i-ch'ang]: "In a time like this, rather than becoming literary stars, you and I would only wish to be the Deaf and the Mute between Heaven and Earth." When Cheng Ch'ao-tsung heard about

this, he laughed and said, "Close your doors, decline all visitors, and amuse yourself with literature. What's the harm?" In recent years, having more free time while staying in mourning, I have collected miscellaneous *hsiao-p'in* by contemporaries and made marginal notes of commentary on them. They are all new and fresh as flower buds, and brilliant in their many and various appearances. They have a rule [*fa*] beyond ordinary rules, a flavor [*wei*] beyond ordinary flavors, and a charm [*yün*] beyond ordinary charms. Exquisite diction and new expressions abound in such writings. They seem to represent the emergence of an extraordinary new fashion since the Lung[-ch'ing] and the Wan[-li] reigns.[15]

Ch'en Chi-ju was right in dating the rise of the *hsiao-p'in* to the Lung-ch'ing (1567–72) and the Wan-li (1573–1620) reigns. The "new fashion," as he called it, took shape as a direct reaction to the domination of the literary stage, starting during the Chia-ching reign (1522–66), by the so-called Later Seven Masters, headed by Li P'an-lung (1514–70) and Wang Shih-chen (1526–90). They carried on the neoclassicist torch of the Earlier Seven Masters, headed by Li Meng-yang (1473–1530) and Ho Ching-ming (1483–1521), in promoting the literary slogan "back to the ancients." Echoing Li Meng-yang's idea to "exclude anything in prose after the Ch'in and Han," Wang Shih-chen expressed his retrogressive concept of literary history in the following observation on the development of literary prose:

The prose of the Western Han had substance. The prose of the Eastern Han became weak, but it had not yet deviated from substance. The prose of the Six Dynasties was pompous: it was deviating from substance. The prose of the T'ang was mediocre, but it remained pompous. The prose of the Sung was clumsy: it was not even pompous anymore, and became more inferior. In the Yüan, there was no prose.[16]

For nearly a century, under the prevailing influence of these two groups, prose writings were loaded with archaic expressions and devoid of emotion in their pale imitation of pre-Han or Han models. Partially because of the political status of these neoclassicists, most of whom were high-ranking courtiers, the influence was so preponderant that it stifled much of the creativeness and originality of artistic instinct. But such intellectual stultification could not last forever, and resistance began to arise in the middle of the Chia-ching reign. It first emerged within the neoclassicist camp itself, from a group of writers later known as belonging to the T'ang-Sung school because, contrary to the argument of Wang Shih-chen and his allies, they acclaimed the prose of the T'ang and the Sung dynasties as their models. Both T'ang Shun-chih (1507–60) and Wang Sheng-chung (1509–59) started by modeling after the prose of the Ch'in and Han dynasties, following contemporary fashion, but in their middle age they turned to the masters of the Sung dynasty, especially Ou-yang Hsiu (1007–72) and Tseng Kung (1019–83). Their close friend Mao K'un (1512–1601) compiled a prose anthology of works by the Eight Prose Masters of the T'ang and the Sung, which quickly gained influence. All three wrote extensive critical works, trying to justify their choice of new models.

In literary practice, however, it was Kuei Yu-kuang* who, though socially unaffiliated with any of the writers of the T'ang-Sung school, most effectively dealt a blow to the theory of the neoclassicists. This was achieved through Kuei's widely acclaimed prose writings as well as his half-century-long pedagogical career, which helped to cultivate a new readership and, consequently, a set of new criteria. Though a lonely schoolteacher before he eventually received the degree of Metropolitan Graduate when he was nearly sixty, Kuei had the courage to challenge Wang Shih-chen's authority. Taking issue with Wang's retrogressive view of prose, Kuei wrote in a preface to his friend Hsiang Ssu-yao's prose collection,

It is hard to talk about the so-called prose of our age. Few engage themselves in learning like the ancients, and as soon as they've found one or two arrogant and mediocre fellows whom they take to be great masters, they flock around to echo their views disparaging writers of previous ages. As Han Yü says,

The writings of Li [Po] and Tu [Fu] survive
And shine in all splendor, far and wide.
They'd never know the dumbness of those kids
Who in vain try to defame their name.
Like ants trying to topple a huge tree,
So laughable are they in overrating themselves!

In the hands of the masters of the Sung and the Yüan, the force of their prose is strong enough to match that of a thousand years ago, while our contemporaries are trying to belittle them like the ants—how deplorable! The one or two arrogant and mediocre fellows who claim to be great masters—aren't they responsible for leading these people astray?[17]

Although Kuei did not mention names, it was known that his reference to "one or two arrogant and mediocre fellows" targeted Wang Shih-chen, widely honored as the leader among men of arts at the time. According to an account provided by Ch'ien Ch'ien-i (1582–1664), an important seventeenth-century critic, after reading this preface Wang Shih-chen said, "I am indeed arrogant, but I'm not mediocre." On hearing the feedback, Kuei remarked again, "One is mediocre exactly because one is arrogant. How could anyone who's arrogant not also be mediocre?"[18] At his death in 1571 Kuei was established as a great prose master of the age. As many of his shorter prose pieces indicate, he was indeed a forerunner of the later *hsiao-p'in* writers. After Kuei Yu-kuang the authority of the neoclassicists was further challenged by various authors toward the end of the sixteenth century, most notably by the eccentric and versatile man of letters Hsü Wei,* the unorthodox thinker Li Chih,* and the great playwright T'ang Hsien-tsu (1550–1616). All three expressed their impatience with the antiquarian and retrogressive ideas of the Later Seven Masters. Li Chih, in particular, lectured and wrote extensively attacking Li P'an-lung and Wang Shih-chen's domination of the literary stage and their negative impact on contemporary literature. His iconoclastic essay "On the Mind of a Child,"* which argues that "all that comes from the mind of a child is excellent writing by itself" and that one should not judge literature "by priority in temporal order," may be considered a raison d'être for the emergence of the new genre.

Under Li Chih's direct influence, the three Yüan brothers Tsung-tao,* Hung-tao, and Chung-tao, while carrying on a heated theoretical debate with the neoclassicists, turned the literary fashion around by their own practice (Chou; Chaves 1978, 1983, 1985). In fact, the new *hsiao-p'in* genre, which could already be found in the writings of Kuei Yu-kuang, Hsü Wei, and T'ang Hsien-tsu, was largely established by the Kung-an school, named after the native town of the Yüan brothers, who found in their experimentation with the form new possibilities of self-expression. The form was further developed by those who joined the camp of the Kung-an school in their denial of the neoclassicists' narrow devotion to pre-Han and Han prose writings as models. Adoption of the new form, which had its prototypes mainly in the prose writings of the Six Dynasties (which Wang Shih-chen had accused of being "pompous" and "deviating from substance") and in the shorter and more casual writings of Su Shih, should therefore be considered as a serious attempt to get free from the straitjacket of the neoclassicist canon.

The Ching-ling school, led by Chung Hsing* and T'an Yüan-ch'un,* which exerted its influence on the literary scene toward the end of the

Wan-li period and especially during the T'ien-ch'i reign (1621–27), has often been misleadingly identified as a mere successor to the Kung-an school. Although Chung and T'an shared common ground with the Yüan brothers in their opposition to the literary theory of the Later Seven Masters, their aesthetics and poetics were in many aspects opposed to those of the Kung-an school. They promoted intricacy and profundity in an attempt to remedy what they regarded as the superficial and vulgar practice of followers of the Yüan brothers. It should be noted here that both the Kung-an and the Ching-ling primarily were schools of poetry and poetics. The *hsiao-p'in* practice of Chung and T'an, in spite of its labored experimentation with diction and syntax, stayed under the influence of the Kung-an school. So did the works of writers such as Ch'en Chi-ju, Wang Ssu-jen, and Li Liu-fang,* who, though not directly affiliated with either of the two groups in the period, nevertheless shared many of their aesthetic and poetic views. As a matter of fact, even T'u Lung,* an ally of Wang Shih-chen's (named by the latter, possibly with a sense of the inevitable doom of neoclassicism, as one of the *Last* Five Masters) and an important neoclassicist critic himself, could not resist the temptation of the Kung-an school in some of his own writings. After all, the inclination to rediscover the charm, comfort, and pleasure in the triviality of civilian life, a major theme of the *hsiao-p'in*, and the struggle for originality and spontaneity in artistic and literary expression were integral parts of the late Ming zeitgeist.

The rise of the *hsiao-p'in*, besides being a reaction against the archaism of the neoclassicists, synchronized with the rise of individualism in the sixteenth century, especially under the rapidly growing posthumous influence of Wang Shou-jen (1472–1529), whose advocacy of the unity of knowledge and action found many followers and sympathizers. This great philosopher's theory of "intuitive knowledge" (*liang chih*) provided a source of inspiration for Li Chih's concept of the "mind of a child" and Yüan Hung-tao's idea of "natural sensibility" (*hsing ling*). In its casualness and spontaneity the *hsiao-p'in* was a proper vehicle for conveying the emotions and idiosyncrasies of the individual.

The *hsiao-p'in* has been accused of being an escapist genre because of its tendency to focus on life's sensual pleasures and triviality. Such characterization is not without its justification. Indeed, as mentioned in Ch'en Chi-ju's above-cited preface to Cheng Ch'ao-tsung's anthology and in the works of quite a few *hsiao-p'in* authors—notably Ch'en Chi-ju, the Yüan brothers, and Li Liu-fang—the form did provide a cathartic outlet, or at least a temporary refuge, where they were able to turn their backs upon the filthy politics of the Wan-li and T'ien-ch'i periods, when corrupt eunuchs seized power in the central court. The late Ming period was, paradoxically, a relatively liberal age in terms of the freedom of artistic and literary expression. Literary inquisition erupted now and then, but was never carried out on such a scale as under the reigns of the early Ming emperors T'ai-tsu (1368–98) and Ch'eng-tsu (1403–24), or as thoroughly as under the reigns of the Ching emperors Yung-cheng (1723–35) and Ch'ien-lung (Goodrich 1935). As long as one did not get personally involved in political and factional strife, one could still afford to do what one liked. *Hsiao-p'in* composition—along with the recreational activities of performing and listening to music, playing board games (Chinese chess and *wei-ch'i*, or *go*), practicing calligraphy, painting, composing poetry, drinking, and flower-watching—became an integral part of the artistic life of late Ming literati.

Last but not least, an ever-increasing demand for reading material—especially that devoted to entertainment—from a social group that expanded dramatically in late sixteenth-century China also accounted for the popularity of the new genre. This group consisted of government school students (*sheng-yüan*) who had passed the preliminary civil service examination and were admitted into county schools, but had not yet acquired the advanced degrees necessary for an official career.[19] It was largely in answer to their need that book printing saw an unprecedented prosperity in the period. The popularity of the *hsiao-p'in* in print accompanied that of other works of popular literature, such as the erotic novel *Golden Lotus* (Chin p'ing mei), the collections of short fiction compiled by Feng Meng-lung (1574–1646?) and Ling Meng-ch'u (1580–1644), and the plays of T'ang Hsien-tsu. Along with these bright stars on the new literary horizon, the *hsiao-p'in* reflected the milieu of late Ming society. Like the famous long Sung scroll *The Ch'ing-ming Festival along the River*, the numerous late Ming *hsiao-p'in* pieces provide a panorama of the bubbling and colorful urban life of the age.

The *Hsiao-p'in* as a Literary Genre

It is extremely difficult to define the generic features of the *hsiao-p'in*. The boundaries of any literary genre can be circumscribed only by the body of works that fall under that generic name, in all their variations and limitations. The *hsiao-p'in* has been compared to the familiar essay, which started with Montaigne in the Western tradition, but there is a quantitative element in the name itself—the term *hsiao* (lit., "little" or "small") prescribes brevity—and most *hsiao-p'in* pieces are much shorter than the Western essay, even though the two forms do share the same great variety of subject and scope. On the other hand, there was no clear standard of length for a piece of *hsiao-p'in*. Under the loose generic name *hsiao-p'in*, all and sundry forms of prose writing were included.

The following groups represent some of the major subjects that were treated in the *hsiao-p'in*. Each had been previously established as a sub-genre of classical Chinese prose with its own history of development. A discussion of how these groups took on new features at the hands of the *hsiao-p'in* may help us to further understand the characteristics of the new form.

Travel Notes

Prototypes of travel notes may be found in the passages describing the landscape (*shan-shui*) in Li Tao-yüan's *A Commentary on the Water Classic*, in personal letters by literati of the Southern Dynasties describing the beauty of nature, and in the descriptions of travel by the great T'ang master Liu Tsung-yüan. The literati of the Eastern Chin regime discovered the beauty of nature when they settled down in the scenic Chiang-nan area. Liu found an outlet for his indignation and sorrow during his exile in the desolate wilderness of Liu-chou (Hargett, pp. 7–69; Nienhauser 1973; Strassberg, pp. 141–47).

In comparison, late Ming writers seem to have rediscovered the beauty of nature, often as a refuge from the ever-worsening political situation and partisan struggles of the age. Their travel notes often carry vivid descriptions of drinking parties held at scenic spots. Compared to earlier travel literature, much of the late Ming *hsiao-p'in* in this category is imbued with more emotion and describes human activity in the scene. There is also a strong sense of spontaneity. As illustrated in Lu Shu-sheng's "A Trip to Wei Village"* and Ch'en Chi-ju's "Trips to See Peach in Bloom,"* the author often made the trip on the impetus of the moment, and sometimes put his experience on record right after the trip. Many such travel notes, as exemplified in those by Wang Ssu-jen, sparkle with humor and wit.

Prefaces and Colophons

Unlike the more formal ones written by the masters of the T'ang and Sung dynasties, prefaces and colophons by late Ming writers often were composed in a casual style, and frequently were written for popular literature rather than for serious classics. For example, when Kuei Yu-kuang wrote a foreword to his "Reflections on *The Book of Documents*,"* he chose to give us an intimate account of his experience of playing with his baby daughter rather than to make serious, scholarly observations on the Confucian classic itself. Ch'en Chi-ju wrote a preface and colophon to *A History of Flowers*,* and Chung Hsing wrote an inscription on *A Drinker's Manual*.* The serious scholarly observation in prefaces and colophons by the T'ang and Sung masters yields its place in the *hsiao-p'in* to description of personal experience or to remarks on life in general.

Life Sketches

Late Ming *hsiao-p'in* writers tended to write about anonymous, obscure figures or their own kinsmen, rather than on the distinguished statesmen and war heroes who dominated earlier biographical literature. For example, Kuei Yu-kuang wrote about his late wife's maidservant ("An Epitaph for Chillyposy"*), and Yüan Hung-tao wrote a biography of the four "stupid but efficient" servants of his family.* However, such authors still had in mind the great model of the genre provided by the Grand Historian Ssu-ma Ch'ien, and tried to achieve similar vividness and forcefulness in their writing.

Personal Letters

Epistolary writing was also a major category of classical Chinese prose with a long history. Late Ming *hsiao-p'in* authors learned from those of the Six Dynasties, but more directly and specifically, they modeled after the informal short epistles of the Sung masters Su Shih and his friend Huang T'ing-chien (1045–1105). Late Ming writers seemed to bear in mind that their letters would probably be further circulated by their addressees to *their* friends and acquaintances, and possibly would be passed down to future generations, as were the letters of Su and Huang, so they seemed always to try to dazzle with, and to show off, their literary talents as well as their mannerisms and idiosyncrasies. Despite this self-consciousness, these letters often breathe of the charisma of their authors. T'u Lung's exquisitely beautiful epistles* represent the very best of the period in their lyrical and vivid expression of the author's personality.

Lin Yutang (1895–1976), who played a crucial role in the recanonization of the *hsiao-p'in* earlier in this century, has defined the *hsiao-p'in wen*, the vernacular belles-lettres prose that flourished in the 1920s and 1930s, as a form in which the author "speaks in an unbuttoned mood." Lin elaborated on this in his essay "The Familiar Style":

> He completely exposes his weakness, and is therefore disarming.
> The relationship between writer and reader should not be one between an austere schoolmaster and his pupils, but one between friends. Only in this way can warmth be generated.
> He who is afraid to use an "I" in his writing will never make a good writer. (1960: 326–27)

The *hsiao-p'in* has been identified as a direct source for the modern vernacular *hsiao-p'in wen*. What Lin said about the latter would appropriately describe the former. In all of the above-mentioned categories, what mark the late Ming *hsiao-p'in* as different from most of their prototypes are strong subjectivity (the ever-present first person singular—"I"), casualness in attitude (the "unbuttoned mood"), a generally informal tone, and frequent use of lively, vernacular expressions. In seeking the "natural sensibility" (*hsing-ling*) that "flows directly from one's heart," as Yüan Hung-tao advocated, late Ming authors generally shied away from archaisms and excessive use of literary allusion. Hence their works are usually characterized by ease and succinctness and demonstrate a clear-cut personal (often idiosyncratic) style, which accounts for, in Ch'en Chi-ju's description, the form's "flavor beyond ordinary flavors" and "charm beyond ordinary charms." Among the various forms of Chinese nonfictional prose, the late Ming *hsiao-p'in* best illustrates Buffon's famous dictum "le style est l'homme même."

The writers who resorted to this new form constituted a small world among themselves, as they generally admired or befriended one another almost in a sense of camaraderie. Hsü Wei, one of the earliest admirers of the art of Kuei Yu-kuang's prose, praised Kuei as "the Master Ou-yang of today."[20] Yüan Hung-tao wrote Hsü Wei's biography ("A Biography of Hsü Wen-ch'ang"*) in enthusiasm. Ch'en Chi-ju, a central cultural figure of the age, was an ardent admirer and young friend of the neoclassicist master Wang Shih-chen, but he also befriended unorthodox peers in the opposite camp, such as the Yüan brothers and Chung Hsing. Ch'en included the *hsiao-p'in* of the elder Lu Shu-sheng and that of T'u Lung in his canon-making big anthology, *The Private Library of Pao-yen Hall* (Pao-yen-t'ang mi-chi), and in so doing should be credited with the preservation of these literary gems. Chung Hsing wrote a colophon to Yüan Hung-tao's calligraphy* and spared no effort in acclaiming the latter's achievement. Wang Ssu-jen admired Hsü Wei and remained a good friend of Yüan Chung-tao's, and his own travel notes received high praise from Ch'en Chi-ju. T'an Yüan-ch'un, Chung Hsing's younger fellow-townsman and close ally, was a friend of Yüan Hung-tao's eldest son and at the latter's request wrote the preface to Hung-tao's *Collected Works*. Late Ming *hsiao-p'in* authors seem to have thrown in their lot with one another and formed an alliance in their common effort to break away from neoclassicist domination.

Chang Tai: The Great Synthesizer of the *Hsiao-p'in*

The entries in Chang Tai's *Dream Memories from the T'ao Hut* represent the highest achievement of the *hsiao-p'in* as an independent literary genre. As its most talented author, Chang Tai deserves more recognition in the West, as much as does the *hsiao-p'in* form itself.[21]

Chang Tai has been glorified by many Chinese literary historians as the genre's greatest author, especially in terms of his synthetic integration of previous styles (Cheng Chen-to IV: 953; Liu Ta-chieh III: 938–41). Indeed, more than any of his predecessors, Chang Tai explored the generic and thematic possibilities of the *hsiao-p'in* and expanded its boundaries.

This is first of all found in the variety of themes in *Dream Memories*, a book that has been glorified as a little classic in its own right ever since the revival of interest in the *hsiao-p'in* in the 1920s. It is not an easy task to categorize or define Chang Tai's book. It may fall under the general category of sketches (*pi-chi*), and probably was influenced by two earlier works, *Notes from the Plum Blossoms Thatched Hut* (Mei-hua ts'ao-t'ang pi-chi) by Chang Ta-fu (1554–1630) and *Notes on Lodge Hill* (Yü shan chu) by Chang Tai's friend and relative by marriage Ch'i Piao-chia (1602–45). However, it differs from most works of its kind in that it overflows with detailed profiles of the author's own life and is impregnated with his emotion and experiences. Placed together, the 122 entries in the eight sections of the work constitute a single book of memoirs of the author's life before the downfall of the Ming imperial reign, yet separately, each of these randomly arranged pieces stands on its own. A more careful look reveals that thematically, the entries fall into the following eight groups: travel notes (on places of historical interest or scenic beauty), family estates, gardening and pets, biographical sketches of friends and acquaintances, festivals and customs, private collections (books, inkslabs, rockeries, etc.), episodes of life in the past, and epicurean pleasures (eating, tea and wine drinking).

Before Chang Tai, no writer had attempted to use the *hsiao-p'in* form to write about such varied themes. In each of these pieces, Chang demonstrates a sharp observation of detail and is always able to present a vivid description of events and objects. Like Marcel Proust's *À la recherche du temps perdu*, the network of visual images, sounds, scents, flavors, and thoughts of Chang Tai's "daydreaming" are interwoven into a fabric of memory and confession. All of the pieces in the book are imbued with a melancholy nostalgia and subtle lyricism that can be found only in the works of writers who had direct personal experience of social upheavals in their lifetime, such as in the later poems of Tu Fu (712–70), written on his exile along the Yangtze in Szechwan after the An Lu-shan rebellion (755), or the song lyrics of loyalist (*yi-min*) poets after the downfall of the Southern Sung in 1279.[22] In *Dream Memories*, as in those poems, one can always discern a sense of contrast, of the wide span of time and space, between past glory and present misery.

The language of Chang Tai's *hsiao-p'in* demonstrates his artistic power in integrating the various styles of his predecessors. The pieces in *Dream Memories* display a resonant lyricism that matches that found in the best of Kuei Yu-kuang. They claim as much liveliness as do the pieces of Yüan Hung-tao, but never the latter's frivolity and occasional crudity. Like Chung Hsing and T'an Yüan-ch'un, Chang Tai was able to make use of archaic expressions, but his prose always runs with ease and grace, and is free from the syntactic "jerkiness" and obscurity of the Ching-ling school. Chang's individual style is closest in spirit to that of his senior friend and fellow Chekiang native Wang Ssu-jen. Both are skillful in integrating vernacular expressions into graceful syntactic structure without ever falling into vulgarity. And it is the same sense of humor and wit, characteristic of Wang Ssu-jen's *hsiao-p'in*, that keeps Chang Tai's sorrowful confessions and memoirs from the pitfall of sentimentality. Above all this, however, shines Chang's individualism.

In the Chinese tradition, the term "great synthesizer" (*chi ta-ch'eng che*) has been reserved for the highest achievement in literary art, such as the *shih* poetry of Tu Fu, the prose of Han Yü (768–824), and (perhaps to a lesser extent) the song lyrics of Chou Pang-yen (1056–1121). To synthesize is to observe, distinguish, choose, absorb, and incorporate various elements and to blend and fuse them into a new unity. It is in this sense that Chang Tai may indeed be ranked as the "great synthesizer" of the late Ming *hsiao-p'in*.

Study of the *Hsiao-p'in*: State of the Field

After the establishment of the Ch'ing empire, the Manchu emperors decided to model after the Han dynasty in reaffirming Confucianism, especially the Neo-Confucian theories of Chu Hsi and the Ch'eng brothers, which stressed conventional moral and ethical values as a means for ideological control. The traditional civil service recruitment examination was reinstituted, and the rigid "eight-legged essay" (*pa-ku wen*) was restored during the early eighteenth century. The perennial literary inquisition silenced intellectuals with an individualist mind and partially accounted for the fact that most leading literati engaged themselves in the study of ancient classics and devoted their entire lives to philological scholarship. The *hsiao-p'in*, which had flourished in the relatively liberal ideological milieu of the late Ming period, dimmed and all but vanished in the next two centuries. The writings of the Kung-an and the Ching-ling schools were in general depreciated and held in contempt by leading writers, many of whom enjoyed imperial patronage. The works of Li Chih in particular, and some of the writings of Hsü Wei, Yüan Hung-tao, and Ch'en Chi-ju, were officially censored. The T'ung-ch'eng school, which emerged on the literary stage in the early eighteenth century and exerted a lasting influence throughout the Ch'ing reign, advocated principles of writing that were frequently opposite in spirit to the *hsiao-p'in*.

It was not until the New Cultural Movement swept throughout China after 1918 that the *hsiao-p'in* was rediscovered and emulated. Chou Tso-jen (1885–1968) identified the late Ming *hsiao-p'in*, especially the ideas of the Kung-an and Ching-ling schools, as a major source of inspiration for the new generation of writers (Pollard). In the 1930s Lin Yutang, as editor-in-chief of a journal that was ironically titled *The Analects* (after the Confucian classic), led a literary campaign of rediscovery and reevaluation of the late Ming *hsiao-p'in*. Volumes of late Ming *hsiao-p'in* that had been suppressed for more than two centuries were reprinted and became instant best-sellers, and many new anthologies were published. The late Ming *hsiao-p'in* was confirmed as a direct predecessor of the new form of short vernacular prose composition, the *hsiao-p'in-wen* (Ch'en Wang-tao).

The outbreak of the Sino-Japanese War in the late 1930s drastically changed the cultural climate in China. The promotion of the *hsiao-p'in*, because of its usually apolitical nature and leisurely tone, began to face opposition from writers on the left. The genre's brief restoration was superseded by another period of suppression during several decades of political cataclysm in China. Lin Yutang came to the United States and introduced the *hsiao-p'in* to the English-speaking public.

In China, after the Communist Party took power in 1949, Lin Yutang was condemned as a "running dog of the American imperialists," Chou Tso-jen remained in obscurity because of his political involvement during the Sino-Japanese War, and the *hsiao-p'in* was branded as a "decadent" and "reactionary" literary form. Not surprisingly in such an atmosphere, scholarship in the field was minimal until the 1980s, when the post-Mao political arena provided a more liberal environment for literary studies. In recent years scholarly books on *hsiao-p'in*, new annotated anthologies, and carefully edited new editions of individual works of late Ming *hsiao-p'in* authors have mushroomed as if with a vengeance.[23]

Across the Taiwan Straits, living under less ideological control, scholars in Taiwan have been able to devote themselves to more serious studies of the genre for a longer period and have provided some of the leading scholarship in the field.[24]

Despite Lin Yutang's pathfinding efforts in introducing the *hsiao-p'in* to the English reader, few serious studies of the genre followed. This is not so surprising, as even today the study of Chinese nonfictional prose in the West lags far behind that of other literary genres such as poetry, fiction, and drama. Between the publication of G. Margouliès's *Le ku-wen chinois* in Paris in 1925 and that of Yu-shih Chen's study of four T'ang and Sung masters of classical prose in 1988, there was virtually no serious study on Chinese nonfictional prose. One may attribute this phenomenon to the philological as well as cultural difficulties of reading Chinese prose. Jordan D. Paper, lamenting the inaccessibility of Chinese prose to the English-reading public, has made a penetrative observation: "A major reason for this vacuum is the inherent difficulty in translating the taut and highly allusive essays into readable English" (p. 67).

On the other hand, the lack of Western scholarship on the genre may also have something to do with the current condition of the study of nonfictional belles-lettres prose in general, which has yet to come of age in the West. Compared to other genres, particularly fiction and poetry, it is a field that literary scholars, from the structuralist to the deconstructionist and beyond, have generally shied away from.[25] Much work is still needed in developing a methodology, a form of critical discourse, in and for this important field.

Individual authors have received more recognition. In 1974 Hung Ming-shui initiated a thorough study of Yüan Hung-tao in his doctoral dissertation at the University of Wisconsin. This was followed in 1978 by Jonathan Chaves's graceful translation, with a fine introduction, of the prose and poems of the three Yüan brothers, which was nominated for the National Book Award in Translation. A few years later, a study of Yüan Hung-tao in French joined the intellectual pursuit.[26] The theories of the Yüan brothers, especially Hung-tao, were made even more accessible to Western academia by the publication of Chih-p'ing Chou's learned monograph in 1988. Studies of Hsü Wei and Li Chih have also appeared in journals and chapters of books, though the former usually concentrate on his artworks, and the latter on his intellectual thought and philosophy.

More recently, three new anthologies—one of travel writing (Strassberg) and two of traditional Chinese literature (Mair; Owen 1996)—have included some *hsiao-p'in* pieces. Owen's anthology has even devoted an entire section to "late Ming informal prose" (pp. 807–33).

The *hsiao-p'in* deserves serious recognition in academia and a wider readership in the West. It should not remain uncharted territory in the ever-growing field of sinological scholarship for too long. It is hoped that this book may make its own little contribution, however modest, toward the further advancement and accessibility of the rich heritage of Chinese nonfictional prose to the Western reader.

Editorial Notes

Selection of *Hsiao-p'in* Texts

This is the first anthology exclusively devoted to presenting the late Ming *hsiao-p'in* in English. In the selection of texts, I have consulted all available Chinese *hsiao-p'in* anthologies but have had to exclude, not without some reluctance, many favorite pieces, as I realized the need to bear the Western reader in mind in the process. In general, I have omitted those that contain too many cultural, historical, and literary allusions and those with which I did not feel fully at ease in translation. Translation is somewhat like a marriage: it won't work if the two sides are not in love.

I also made special efforts to include those that were not available in English. However, a few exceptions, due to their great literary merit, deserve the perennial competition of "the blossoming of a hundred flowers" in translation.

Two essays, Li Chih's "On the Mind of a Child" and Yüan Hung-tao's "A Biography of Hsü Wen-ch'ang," can hardly be classified as *hsiao-p'in*: both are somewhat too formal in style and serious in tone. Nevertheless, due to the importance of the former and the possible interest to our reader of the latter, they have been included along with traditional *hsiao-p'in* by their respective authors.

Translation

Yen Fu (1853–1921), one of the most prominent Chinese translators in history, set down the goals of translation in three words: "accuracy" or "fidelity to the original" (*hsin*); "intelligibility" (*ta*); and, last but by no means least, "elegance in style" (*ya*). Despite the perennial academic discussions on translation and its theory and practice, Yen Fu's criteria still stand out to this translator as the highest goal one can ever hope to achieve.

When one thinks about the translation of the *hsiao-p'in* in English, the great pathfinder who immediately comes to mind is Lin Yutang, who surely achieved Yen Fu's criteria of intelligibility and elegance, though not infrequently at the cost of fidelity. The late James J. Y. Liu, in a rare observation on translation, identified among various schools of translation a group that he called the "scholar-translators," who would place "fidelity" firmly in first place. I venture to classify *Vignettes from the Late Ming* as belonging to this type. In my childhood, when I was learning my English, I sometimes ran into one of those texts, popular in China then, in which the original was printed side by side with the translation. In such texts, even the slightest deviation from the original hardly escapes the attention of a meticulous reader. In the process of translation, I often had those texts in mind and hope that this work can stand the test of the harsh critical eye of such a reader.

However, with such eminent translators as Lin Yutang and, more recently, Jonathan Chaves and Richard E. Strassberg in mind, I have also tried my best to stick to Yen Fu's other two standards. In so doing, my life-long fondness for and enthusiastic reading of the English essay has proved invaluable. Difficult as it is, I have tried to convey the various styles of the Chinese authors in this anthology, just as great variety of style is evident among English essay masters such as Francis Bacon, William Hazlitt, Charles Lamb, Thomas De Quincey, John Ruskin, Walter Pater, and G. K. Chesterton. I dare not claim that I have achieved that goal in this book, but I have indeed tried my best.

Classical Chinese texts do not use paragraphs. The paragraphing in the translation is therefore based upon the translator's understanding. On some occasions, words or phrases that are not in the original have been added in order to make the text comprehensible. They are placed in square brackets.

Introductory Notes

An introductory note with biographical information and brief critical comments precedes the selections by each author. These notes are based primarily upon the biographies (whenever available) from the officially authorized *History of the Ming* (Ming-shih), first published in 1739, but I have also incorporated into them reading from all and sundry sources, including the works of these authors. Readers who want to know more may find more detailed and longer biographies in the works edited by L. Carrington Goodrich and Chao-ying Fang, Arthur W. Hummel, and William Nienhauser.

Annotations

Annotations are provided to help the reader better understand the literary allusions and cultural context. For the preparation of these annotations I have relied on two Chinese dictionaries, *Tz'u yüan* (Hong Kong: Commercial Press, rev. ed., 1980) and *Tz'u hai* (Shanghai: Shanghai tz'u-shu ch'u-pan-she, 1980), as well as other lexica.

Romanization

The traditional Wade-Giles romanization system for Chinese names is used in this book, as the editor believes it still is more accessible to what Virginia Woolf called an English-speaking "common reader." The *pinyin* system, officially used in the People's Republic of China and recently gaining ground among Western sinologists, was not designed with the average English reader in consideration and contains several syllables whose pronunciation is difficult to estimate. Deviations from this transliteration system have been made for names that have long been familiar in their nonstandard form to Western readers, such as the Latinized names Confucius and Mencius, and Li Po (rather than Li Pai). For some well-known geographical names I have used traditional Anglicized "post office" names (e.g., Peking, Yangtze).

Chinese Nomenclature

In Chinese nomenclature, family name comes first in order. Educated Chinese were given two personal names, a formal name (*ming*) and a "style" (*tzu*). The latter was traditionally adopted for use at the "capping ceremony" when one reached the age of twenty. A scholar would also assume a cognomen (*hao*), sometimes even several. It was a lasting fashion in the writings of the literati to address people by their "styles" and cognomens, or sometimes by the highest official title they had held. Take the case of "China's greatest poet" for an illustration: He was born in the Tu family and was given the formal name of Fu. But, in the numerous writings about him, he was referred to mostly by his "style" (Tzu-mei), his cognomen (Shao-ling—the complete form of which was the "Old Rustic of Shao-ling"), or by his official affiliation, Kung-pu (lit., "Ministry of Works," where Tu Fu served as vice-director). To prevent needless confusion for the Western reader, most "styles" and cognomens have been converted into formal names in translation.

Official Titles

For most of the traditional Chinese official titles, I have followed the excellent scholarship of the late Charles O. Hucker (1919–94) in his magnum opus, *A Dictionary of Official Titles in Imperial China*.

Measurements

Chinese measurements of length, area, weight, and volume have been converted to their closest Western equivalents, whenever possible, with the exception of occasional rhetorical usage. Traditional Chinese measurements varied in time and place, but in general grew slightly in size over the centuries. Conversions should therefore be regarded as no more than approximate values and in the context of earlier periods should be adjusted downward a little.

Years

For the designation of years, the traditional Chinese calendar used two sets of signs, the Heavenly Stems and the Earthly Branches, with one being taken from each set and combined to form sixty pairs. Those used in these essays have been converted into their Western equivalents, but due to the Chinese lunar calendar, they do not correspond to each other exactly. Readers who need to find the exact date in Western calendars (Julian until 1582 and Gregorian thereafter) may consult Keith Hazelton, *A Synchronic Chinese-Western Daily Calendar, 1341–1661* A.D. (Minneapolis: University of Minnesota Press, 1984).

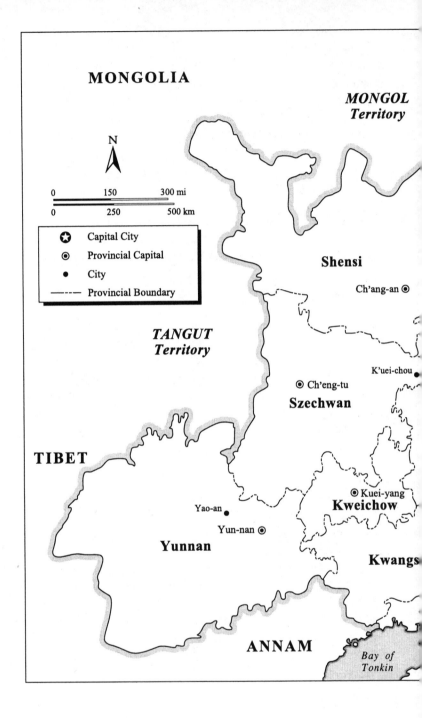

MONGOLIA

N

| 0 | 150 | 300 mi |
| 0 | 250 | 500 km |

★ Capital City
◉ Provincial Capital
● City
----- Provincial Boundary

MONGOL
Territory

Shensi

Ch'ang-an ◉

TANGUT
Territory

K'uei-chou ●

◉ Ch'eng-tu

Szechwan

TIBET

◉ Kuei-yang

Kweichow

Yao-an ●

Yun-nan ◉

Yunnan

Kwangs

ANNAM

Bay of
Tonkin

The Ming Empire

MANCHU
Territory

•Hsüan-fu
✪Shun-t'ien
(Peking)
Northern
Metropolitan
Region

'ai-yüan ◉

Shansi
•Shun-te
◉ Chi-nan
Shantung
•Yen-chou

KOREA

YELLOW SEA

Kaifeng ◉

Honan
•Nan-yang

Southern
Metropolitan
Region
Yangchow•
Ying-t'ien ✪
(Nanking)
Soochow•
Sung-chiang•

ang-yang•

hing-chou•
◉ Wu-chang

Hangchow ◉
Shao-hsing•

Chekiang

EAST CHINA
SEA

Hu-kuang
◉ Nan-ch'ang

Kiangsi

Fu-chou◉

Fukien

Taiwan

Kuei-lin ◉

Kwangtung
◉ Kuang-chou

SOUTH CHINA
SEA

Literature is landscape on our desk;
landscape is literature on the earth.

—Chang Ch'ao
Reflections of Profound Dreams (late 17th cent.)

Here is a handful of chosen flowers,
a dinner of exquisite little courses,
a bunch of variously coloured air balloons.

—Virginia Woolf (1918)
on Logan Pearsall Smith's *Trivia*

Vignettes from the Late Ming

Kuei Yu-kuang (1507–71)

A native of K'un-shan County in the Southern Metropolitan Region (which later was divided into Kiangsu and Anhwei in the Ch'ing dynasty), Kuei Yu-kuang won first place in the county examination when he was twenty years old and received the degree of Provincial Graduate with second-place honor in 1540. But during the next two dozen years, he failed eight times consecutively at the national examinations, held every three years in the capital. During this time he earned his living as a private tutor preparing young men for the examinations and saw many of his students succeed. Nevertheless he managed to make a national name for himself through his pedagogic activities—by his cognomen "Master of Cheng-ch'uan"—as the leading prose writer of the age. When he finally won the degree of Metropolitan Graduate in 1565, he was nearly sixty years old. He was then appointed as magistrate of Ch'ang-hsing County, where he practiced a policy of benevolence, reducing as much as he could the official business of litigation. Unappreciated by his superiors, he was transferred in 1569 to become assistant prefect of Shun-te Prefecture, with the specified assignment of managing the government horse stables and pasturage, during the term of which office he wrote several essays on the history of horse culture. The next year, he was promoted to the position of assistant director of the Court of the Imperial Stud in Nanking, but actually stayed in the capital to manage the Proclamations Office of the Grand Secretariat, where he was assigned the task of drafting an official record of the late Emperor Chia-ching. Kuei was enthusiastic about the assignment because he had finally become an imperial historian like his idol, Ssu-ma Ch'ien, the "Grand Historian" of the Han dynasty. The position placed the imperial library collection of the Grand Secretariat within his reach and provided him an opportunity to demonstrate his literary and historiographical talents. But destiny played a cruel joke—within half a year Kuei suddenly fell ill and soon passed away, before he could complete any significant work of history.

However, at his death he left behind more than three hundred prose pieces, and his reputation as a great master had been established. Despite an earlier verbal war between them, Wang Shih-chen, a towering literary figure in sixteenth-century China, hailed Kuei as "one in a millennium," after Han Yü and Ou-yang Hsiu, two great prose masters respectively of the T'ang and Sung dynasties. During the next century, his fame was further promoted by leading men of letters. Ch'ien Ch'ien-i collaborated with Kuei's great-grandson Kuei Chuang (1613–73) in compiling the complete edition of Kuei Yu-kuang's work, a classified collection in forty-one sections. Huang Tsung-hsi (1610–95) called Kuei's prose writings representive of the very best of the Ming dynasty. Two centuries after his death Kuei was canonized by writers of the T'ung-ch'eng school (which was most influential in the middle of the Ch'ing dynasty) not only as the greatest prose writer of the Ming, but also as the singular linkage between the Eight Prose Masters of the T'ang and the Sung and themselves.

The inclusion of Kuei Yu-kuang in our anthology will make some traditional Chinese literary historians turn in their graves. Kuei has always been honored as a master of formal "classical prose" (ku-wen), the generic principles of which were in many aspects opposite to those of the casual hsiao-p'in. He learned the secret of his descriptive and narrative art from various models of different ages, but especially from Ssu-ma Ch'ien. At his best he was able to combine it with a rich underlying lyricism, which he probably learned from Ou-yang Hsiu. In many of his shorter prose pieces he confided in us, like an intimate friend sitting by the fireside, the little joys and sorrows of daily life and the uncertainty and vicissitudes of human relations with delicacy, vividness, and depth of emotion. Although the term hsiao-pin never occurred to Kuei Yu-kuang, his prose pieces often display, as our selection here indicates, the randomness and spontaneity, as well as a penchant for triviality, that characterize the genre.

Foreword to "Reflections on *The Book of Documents*"

In 1531, during the Chia-ching reign, I was back from the Southern Capital[1] after having failed in the examination. I lived in seclusion behind closed doors. Few of my old friends ever dropped by. There was no spare room in the house. I had to stay in the inner chambers in daytime and amused myself holding my baby daughter in arms day in and day out. When she fell asleep, or while she was being breast-fed by her mother, I would read *The Book of Documents*.[2] My baby also liked to have fun with books. When she saw a book, she would often move her fingers along the lines and make some sound in her mouth, as if she understood it well enough. So I often managed to go on with my reading, and when I had an idea, I would make a note of it. Whenever something crossed my mind, I had to grab my writing brush in a hurry. As someone in the past said, "The eagle swoops down when the hare stirs."[3] Unable to find the leisure to work these notes into essays, I kept them in my suitcase for possible future use. As regards structural analyses and syntactic explication, we already have those masters in old times, and I wouldn't dare to compare my notes to theirs, so I titled mine simply "Reflections on *The Book of Documents*."

I often think that reading a book is like an artisan drawing a portrait. He paints the ears, the eyes, the mouth, the nose: some big, some small, some fat, some thin. Every part may resemble its original; yet when people see the portrait, they may feel that it doesn't look like the person. If that is the case, the artisan must have acquired the shape but lost the spirit! I dare not claim to have grasped the spirit in my reading, but I have always tried to search for it.

A Parable of Urns

A man put an urn by the roadside. The urn tumbled on the ground and broke. The man was about to leave, when another person with an urn in hand passed by. The man went up and grabbed the other person, saying, "Why did you break my urn?" Then he seized the latter's urn and gave him his own broken one. Most of the people in the street sided with the man who broke his urn in the first place, and eventually the person who passed by with an urn, being unable to defend himself, had to leave without his urn.

Oh, my! If the man who broke his urn had not seen anyone passing by, he would have left. But the person who passed by with an urn was unfortunate enough to have run into him and, as a result of that, received a broken urn in exchange for his unbroken one. To get an unbroken urn in exchange for a broken one: this is the way an incident may fluctuate. As for the people in the street, they must have lost their minds!

5

Inscription on the Wall of the Wild Crane Belvedere

In the spring of 1538, during the Chia-ching reign, my friends and I had a gathering for essay composition at the Wild Crane Belvedere.

Horse Saddle Hill in our K'un-shan County, though small, does have a spectacular view. The belvedere stands at the foot of the hill. There is a fountain spring by its side, the water of which is clear and sweet, very nice to drink. Toward the east, where big rocks abound, there is the part of the hill that commands the best view, locally known as Eastern Cliff or Liu Lung-chou's Grave, as Liu Kuo of the Sung is buried there.[1] The grave is among a tangle of rocks. Looking upward from the grave, one sees nothing but a dark, undulating sheet of greenness. There is only a little path winding up by the side of the stone cliff; no one can tell where it leads to. It is believed that some immortals might live up there.

The belvedere was first built by Yang Tzu-ch'i, alias Ming-fu, of Tz'u-hsi. Ming-fu was known as a magistrate who, unlike ordinary officials, was fond of literature and enjoyed the company of men of letters. Now the place is honored as a shrine for Ming-fu. My goodness! How could Ming-fu have ever known that people like us would hold a gathering here more than forty years later? The party was started by six people and joined by two latecomers. Pan Shih-ying, who had come all the way from Chia-ting, brought water from the fountain to make tea and assumed the role of the host. We left one by one, but Shih-ying and his friend stayed there. The wind was strong, the rain heavy, the cliff cracked, and pieces of stones rolled down. Wild animals in the hills screamed at night. How scary it must have been for them!

The Craggy Gazebo

Some twenty-two miles by boat from the city of K'un-shan, on the Wu-sung River, is a place named An-t'ing. According to the local atlas, there used to be a certain An-t'ing River, which is nowhere to be seen today. It is a place shunned by people in the county due to its poor soil and the incivility of the locality. But it is where my wife's family lives, and I, for one, enjoy the serenity inside the house. In this year of 1542, I have engaged myself in reading here.

West of the house are some old trees, a clear pool, and a rocky hill. There is a gazebo on the hill. Up there one can glimpse the Wu-sung River circling and winding toward the east, the wind-filled sails that flit past deserted villages and treetops, and, right ahead, the nine peaks of Mount Hua-t'ing and the ancient Buddhist temple and pagoda at Green Dragon Town. The gazebo did not have a name in the past, so I have named it Craggy.

As said in the *Chuang-tzu*,[1] Keng-sang Ch'u, after having learned about the Tao from Lao-tan,[2] lived in Craggy Hills. Among his retainers, those who were smart left him. Among his maidservants, those who were noble-hearted kept their distance from him. Only the thick-witted stayed with him; only the slovenly served under him. Three years later, there was a big harvest at Craggy. Local residents worshipped him as a god, said prayers, and offered sacrifices to him.

Now I live here behind closed doors all day long. Occasionally, a friend or two visits me from faraway, and we sing and chant together among brambles. My wife owns a little more than six and a half acres of land. There happened to be a big drought this year. By driving ox carts day and night to water the fields, we had a pretty nice crop, and we brewed several piculs[3] of wine. In the chilly wind, the leaves have turned yellow and fallen to the ground. I call out to my boys to get me some wine, climb up to the gazebo, and cry out aloud in ecstasy: Who were those who left me and kept their distance from me? Who are those who stay with me and serve under me? And who will be those who worship me as a god, say prayers, and offer sacrifices to me?

I have hereby written this note about the Craggy Gazebo.

The Hsiang-chi Belvedere

The Hsiang-chi Belvedere[1] was formerly called the Southern Pavilion. It was less than twelve feet square, just the size for one person to live in. An old shed about a hundred years in age, it was penetrated by dust and dirt, and when it rained, water would seep in. I used to try to relocate the desk and yet, looking around, could not find a dry spot for it. Also, the room faced north and therefore did not get any sunshine; as soon as noontime passed, it would grow dark inside.

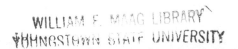

I made a few repairs. First I stopped the leak in the ceiling, installed four windows in the front, and had a wall facing the sun in the south built around the courtyard. Now the sunshine is reflected into the room from the wall, brightening the room. I also planted in the courtyard orchid, cassia, bamboo, and some trees, which enhance the grace of the old balustrades and thresholds. Then I filled up the shelves with books. Now it has become a place where I may sit back or lie down, to chant or sing aloud. Often I sit alone in silence, and nature presents its myriad sounds against the quiet all around the courtyard. Little birds frequently come to peck at food, and do not leave even when people approach them. On the fifteenth of the lunar month, the bright moon lights up half of the wall, and the shadow of the cassia trees spreads out in a fine pattern. When a wind arises, the shadow stirs. A lovely sight indeed.

And yet for all the time I have lived here I hold as many happy memories as sad ones. The courtyard used to open to both the north and the south as one unit. When my father and uncles started living separately, small gates and walls were erected here and there, both in and out of the house. Dogs east and west barked at one another. Visitors had to pass through the kitchen to get to dinner. Roosters stayed in the front hall. The courtyard was first separated by fences and then by walls. Thus the look of the house has changed twice already.

An old nanny in the family used to live here. She was the maid of my late grandmother. Having been the nanny for two generations, she was well treated by my late mother. The shed was formerly connected on its western side to the inner chambers. My mother sometimes would come over here. The nanny would often tell me, "This was the place where your mother used to stand." She would also say, "Your elder sister was crying loudly in my arms. Your mother tapped at the door with her fingers, asking, 'Is the baby feeling cold? Or is she hungry?' And I would talk back to her from behind the door." Before she finished saying this, I started weeping, and the nanny also cried.

After I had my hair tied up,[2] I often read my books at the belvedere. One day, grandmother dropped by and said, "Sonny, I've hardly seen you for a long time. Why are you staying here all day long, almost as quiet as a young lady?" As she was leaving, she murmured to herself when she closed the door, "It has been a long time since the family had any success in studies. Maybe we can expect this boy to accomplish something." In a short while she was back again, holding an ivory court tablet[3] in her hand. She said, "This was held in his hands by my grandfather, Chamberlain for Ceremonial, when he went to court during the Hsüan-te reign.[4] Some day you should be the one to use it." Looking around at all the relics, it seems as if what took place then happened only yesterday; I can't help crying out loud and long.

East of the belvedere there used to be the kitchen, and people on their way there would pass by the belvedere. Having stayed inside behind closed doors for a long time, I was able to tell who it was by listening to the sound of the footsteps. The belvedere caught fire four times, but it never burned down, as if it were protected by divinity.

Master Hsiang-chi observed, "Widow Ch'ing of Shu held her place at the cinnabar mine, and made it the most profitable place in the world. Later the emperor of Ch'in had a tower erected in her memory.[5] When Liu Pei and Ts'ao Ts'ao fought each other for the state, Chu-ko Liang rose to power from Lung-chung.[6] But when these two lived in obscurity in remote places, how was it possible for the world to know their talent? Now this humble gentleman here, who lives in this shabby belvedere, raises his eyebrows, looks all around, and believes that he commands spectacular views. Those who hear of this may wonder what difference there is between him and the frog down in the well."[7]

Five years after I wrote the above note, my wife came to this house after our marriage. She would often come over to the belvedere to ask me about things in ancient times, or lean over the desk to practice calligraphy. Once, when my wife came back from visiting her parents, she told me what her little sisters had said to her: "Sister, we've heard that there is a pavilion at your house. Now what is a pavilion?" Six years later, my wife died. The belvedere turned into a wreck. Another two years later, I had nothing to do after being sick for a long time, so I had the Southern Pavilion fixed again. The structure now has become slightly different from before. Yet since then I have stayed away from home most of the time, and hardly live there anymore.

In the courtyard there is a loquat tree that my wife planted by herself in the year she passed away. It stands tall now, with its foliage spreading out like a canopy.

An Epitaph for Chillyposy

The girl was my wife Lady Wei's maid. She died on the fourth day of the fifth lunar month in 1537, during the Chia-ching reign, and was buried on a small hill. She served us, but not to the end. Wasn't it all destiny?

When the girl first came over at my wedding, she was only ten years old. Her hair was tied in two hanging knots, and she dragged around in a dark-green cotton skirt. One day, it was very cold. We made a fire and cooked some water chestnuts over it. The girl peeled them, filling up a small earthen pot. When I entered the room from outside, I picked up some to eat, but the girl took the pot away and would not give me any more, which set Lady Wei laughing. My wife often told her to lean at the side of our little table to eat her meal. Whenever the meal was about to be served, she would roll her eyes around slowly in her sockets, and my wife would point it out to me for a chuckle.

Looking back upon those days, I suddenly realized that ten years have passed. Alas, woe is me!

Lu Shu-sheng (1509–1605)

Lu Shu-sheng was born into a poor family in Hua-t'ing in the prefecture of Sung-chiang, Southern Metropolitan Region, and brought up working as a farmhand, but he grabbed every chance to read and educate himself during breaks from his work in the fields. The diligence paid off: in 1541 he won first place in the capital examination, was immediately admitted into the imperial Han-lin Academy, and later was appointed as an imperial historian. From then on Lu received many senior official appointments, but declined or resigned from most of them. In the remaining six decades of his life (he lived to the venerable age of ninety-six), his years in officialdom totaled only about a dozen. When Emperor Shen-tsung succeeded to the throne, Lu entered the cabinet as minister of rites at insistent imperial demand. However, his term lasted less than a year. Probably because of his indignation at the eunuchs' manipulation of court politics, he made repeated requests to be pensioned off and was eventually granted permission. He once told his son, who won the degree of Metropolitan Graduate in 1589, not to seek any central government appointment.

Lu befriended many younger poets and writers. Ch'en Chi-ju, a close friend and fellow native of Hua-t'ing, wrote in a biographical note that even at the age of eighty-six, Lu wrote to invite him to join in a trip to White Dragon Pool. Ch'en noted with great admiration how the old man could walk up and down a storied pavilion without using his walking stick, fast and robust like a young man. Lu also told Ch'en that every night, before bedtime, he would walk a thousand paces before retiring.

Ch'en Chi-ju printed several collections of Lu Shu-sheng's prose pieces in The Private Library of Pao-yen Hall, *a book series of miscellaneous writings that included many volumes of* hsiao-p'in. *Rich in literary allusions, Lu's vignettes often breathe a sense of humor and a cheerful appreciation of life's little pleasures.*

Inkslab Den

I have few hobbies. All my life, except for books, I have not collected any "superfluous thing."[1] When I served as an imperial historian, I obtained a Tuan inkslab.[2] When I was an official at Nan-yung, I obtained another inkslab, made of She stone.[3] In a number of years I got several kinds of inkstone. Having instructed some craftsmen to work on them, I acquired ten inkslabs altogether. I told myself, "These are quite enough for a collection. I should not get any more than ten." So I gave myself a cognomen, Master of Ten Inkslabs. I put them in a cabinet, which I named Inkslab Den. From time to time I would take them out, place them on the table, and sit there, facing them, in great pride. A friend of mine reproved me for my obsession with them. I responded, "Isn't such an obsession better than one with some other things?"

One day a friend who had an eye for inkslabs examined them and found that none was of superb quality. I said, "My friend, you know I am obsessed with inkslabs. Why should I be obsessed with superb ones only? Besides, there has already been much discussion of inkslabs. Ou-yang Hsiu, Ts'ai Hsiang, and Hung Kuo believed that some of the good ones among the Dragon-tail are superior to the Tuan inkstone.[4] But Su Shih argued to the contrary, and even elaborated on it in his writings. Perhaps there is simply no fixed value for things, and their worth is to be decided only through the mouths of the literati? In that case, how can anyone know whether those in my collection are superb or not? If, in my hobby of collecting inkslabs, I'll take nothing but the very best ones, then among rare antiques in the world, aren't there a myriad things other than inkslabs? As for rare antiques, men in power can surely acquire them, but often they have to snatch them from the possession of others. Therefore I will not give up my preference for any other hobby. Lacking in both talent and refinement, I do take a fancy to inkslabs, and yet have no idea how to treasure them. I am indeed not worthy of treasuring inkslabs, so how am I supposed to be able to consider the superiority or inferiority of their quality? However, I will not replace my hobby of collecting inkslabs with one of collecting rare antiques. Thus, by staying in my favor, perhaps these inkslabs have indeed been treasured accordingly? So, my obsession will stay unchanged."

The other day, while my son, Chang, was practicing calligraphy, I took out one of my inkslabs and gave it to him, saying, "When you become a good calligrapher, I'll give you the entire den." Someone asked [if he could also have some], and I said, "These are the 'black felt blanket'[5] in my house. Please don't regard them as bags of gold."

The above was written by Master of Ten Inkslabs.

Bitter Bamboo

Bamboos abound in the Chiang-nan area,[1] and local residents eat bamboo shoots from habit. In springtime, when the new bamboos emerge from the soil, the sprouting shoots are picked for food. They are steamed, boiled for soup, or placed on the menu as a vegetable dish. Busybodies eyeing them for their delicate flavor think nothing of harming their potential growth. For this reason, while bamboos are well protected by their masters in beautiful, lush gardens behind winding walls and locked doors, the same people spare no effort in cutting them down when they want to eat them. Only the shoots of those that are not edible on account of a bitter flavor are spared from being cut down. Those that are ignored and allowed to grow on their own along mountain streams, in valleys, or by rocks are abandoned because of their bitter flavor, while all of the better-tasting ones are picked and sometimes are eliminated entirely.

Things that taste good get themselves destroyed accordingly; those that are bitter, though cast aside, are spared. Since everyone likes savory things, things that taste bitter remain unharmed. In this world, everyone values things of use and ignores those of no use. Will anyone ever know the misery of things that are picked for use, and the bliss of those that are left alone? Are they not like what Chuang-tzu called "those who make use of their uselessness"? In the southwestern corner of my executive mansion, a grove of bamboos has grown out of cracked bricks. Unlike those behind winding walls and locked doors, they can equal only those that grow on their own along mountain streams, in valleys, or by rocks. However, they don't have to worry about being cut down. They will stay whole and secure from danger because of their bitter taste. Some visitors looked down upon them as bitter bamboos. I happened to be reading Chuang-tzu, and I found his words quite refreshing. On reflection, I've written the above note.

A Trip to Wei Village

M̲r. Wang, director of the Bureau of Waterways, invited us to make a trip to Wei Village. On the day before, in intense summer heat, at a party at the house of Mr. Yang, the supervising secretary, we had made an appointment to make the trip together.

I got up in the morning. The sun was struggling behind dark clouds. I sent a clerk to hurry Mr. Yang. In a short while Mr. Yang arrived on horseback and asked me to join him. On our way, a drizzle was suddenly over us. Servant boys followed holding two big umbrellas in their hands. We went out of the Ts'ung-wen Gate[1] and traveled south for about a mile and a half when the rain turned heavy, so we stopped and just stayed on horseback for a while. To our right, we could see a round mound where the trees were half hidden beyond the boundless mist and clouds. Looking backward, the city wall emerged from out of the heavy fog. I turned to Mr. Yang and said, "This is really the picture for Assistant Director Wang's line 'The imperial city in clouds.'[2] Who would ever have grasped its essence, if not the two of us, out of our curiosity?"

We moved a little farther southward and then turned left. The narrow footpath, among grass and trees, barely allowed one horse to pass through at a time, so we gave up the umbrellas and asked a servant to pull the horse in front. The two of us bent over on horseback. The rain and the wet leaves were all over us, dampening our clothes.

After a little while we arrived. We entered the gate, unfastened our belts, and sat down by the northern door. A cool wind blew through the room. Thinly clad, I stood up, away from my seat. Mr. Yang smiled and stared at me, saying, "You don't have the stamina to stand this?" So he told the servants to close one of the door leaves.

We sat there for a long time before the rain stopped. Then we walked around the vegetable garden and went to the gazebo by the pond. The gazebo was right in front of the pond, which was about an acre or two in area. The lotus that had just come into bloom covered the surface of the water. Slender willows provided their shade over the embankment. It very much resembled Chiang-nan.

After we sat for a while, the host arrived and offered us drinks in large goblets. By then, there was a little sunshine. The servants reported that it was noontime. A light wind fanned away the heat, and steam rose from the drying rainwater. I sat on the left, facing the wind. Turning to the two gentlemen, I said, "This is T'ao Yüan-ming's old friend, and I am sitting face to face with him on my side."[3] We raised our goblets and toasted one another. Then we moved over to the house in the front, but after a few rounds of drink we moved back to the gazebo. Tossing down our drink from raised goblets, we talked about the scenic spots of each of our native towns.

At sunset we took a walk to the Buddhist temple, where we had a little rest in the abbot's room. While we were sipping some tea there, we heard the soft rumbling of distant thunder, so the three of us rode home together. When we looked back at where we had been, it was already hidden in the dark.

On that day we made the trip in the rain, which was quite unusual. The guests arrived first and waited a long time for the host: quite unusual. We did not play any chess at the party: quite unusual. I had been unwell and usually did not go to parties, and if I took a ride it was within one-third of a mile in distance. On that day I rode for six or seven miles round-trip, and after a whole day of traveling with the two gentlemen, I was still able to take up my writing brush and put it on record at night. That's quite unusual, too!

A Short Note about My Six Attendants in Retirement

In the year I turned seventy, a Buddhist monk from Mount T'ien-t'ai presented to me a rattan cane. I still had strong legs then, and would not use it for any distance within a hundred steps. When I was eighty, a friend who returned from overseas gave me as a gift a wooden cane. Within its close texture, there appears quite abruptly a grain like that of the joint of a crane's leg, which spreads from top to bottom like a string of beads. I believe that it could have been made from only a very old tree that had gone through much frost and snow. In between having these two, I got myself three bamboo canes, all of light weight and easy to carry along. I often used one on my regular walk and relied much on it. In recent years the mountain recluse Chang, back from a trip to Yen and Chao,[1] gave me a heavy and sturdy black wooden cane, saying, "You need this for sightseeing in the mountains."

Old and feeble now, I have already given up all my early ambitions to visit the Five Sacred Mountains[2] in my life. Although my mind still wanders to faraway places, I am too weak to climb or to wade anymore. So I can only place these canes by my seat all the time. Occasionally I would hold one in my hands and look at it, and let my imagination soar beyond the colorful clouds. Isn't this almost like what Tsung Ping called "recumbent travel"?[3] Hence I put down here, as I now have some free time, an account of how and in what order these six came into my possession.

These days I really rely on these six attendants to support and entertain myself in old age. In my senility I am like the morning star, or the dew at sunrise: how much more time do I still have to move around with my attendants? I cannot help feeling melancholy about it. So I write down a few more words with the "worn-out draperies" and the "dropped hairpins" in mind.[4] Some may say that these six attendants will perhaps become immortalized because of me, but that's not what I'm able to know.

Inscription on Two Paintings in My Collection

Chung Ch'in-li was a leading painter of our dynasty. Ch'in-li's paintings belong to the category of "fine brushwork,"[1] and he was especially good at cattle painting, the spirit and style of which almost equal the works of Tai Sung and Han Huang.[2] His paintings were more recent in time, and he painted quite a lot, so they are not yet treasured in the world. But among fellow painters his works are already held in superior rank.

These two square pieces of mine I got from Mr. Yeh of White Cliff, when I was still under twenty. I often look at them and enjoy the free flow and vitality of the brush strokes and the use of ink, and the striking resemblance to reality. I adore and prize them, have them wrapped up and placed in a suitcase, and from time to time take them out for a look.

In the year 1541, when I made a trip to the capital with great expectations for my accomplishments, these also went in my company. In the boat, during the journey, in wind and rain, by dusk or dawn, under lamplight or by fireside, whenever I had some leisure in the intervals between writing, I would always take them out and set them in front of me.

It often occurs to me that people in the past were not always able to keep in their possession the paintings they valued. Yet these have been in my company for nearly twenty years and have not yet been snatched away by some busybody. I have hereby written this note so that it may have a chance to be passed on along with Han Yü's note on figure painting[3]—who knows?

Inscription on a Portrait of Tung-p'o
Wearing Bamboo Hat and Clogs

When he was still in court in his official cap and gown, his contemporaries raged and raved, and turned their backs on him. When he looks like a mountaineer and is dressed like a rustic, everyone takes pleasure in catching sight of him. That person then was a Tung-p'o; this one now is also a Tung-p'o. Come to think about all this, viewers, why not chuckle on Tung-p'o's behalf?[1]

Hsü Wei (1521–93)

Hsü Wei, a native of Shan-yin in the prefecture of Shao-hsing, Chekiang, was well known for his talent even when he was only a student at the prefectural school, but he failed in all subsequent attempts at the higher civil service examinations. He became a private secretary and protégé of Hu Tsung-hsien (1511–65), the powerful governor of Chekiang and supreme commander of troops in the southeastern provinces, and became the latter's consultant in his military maneuvering against the Japanese pirates and other insurgents in the region. Hsü enjoyed Hu's trust and stayed with him until the latter was impeached and dismissed in 1562. Three years later, after Hu was arrested and died in prison, Hsü began to live in fear of being implicated, and made several attempts to kill himself. In a fit of madness he killed his wife, was imprisoned, and was sentenced to death. After seven years of confinement, he was released in 1573 after repeated appeals on his behalf from officials who knew and admired him. In 1576 he went to serve as a private secretary of the Grand Coordinator of Hsüan-fu Prefecture on the northern frontier, but after only one year there he came back south. For the rest of his life Hsü earned a living by writing and painting, and often lived under the roof of a student or an admirer as a houseguest.

Hsü Wei was one of the most colorful Ming intellectuals. His life and works—which might remind a Western reader of someone like Oscar Wilde or Vincent van Gogh—provide a rare sample from Chinese cultural history for a study of "art and madness." A versatile artist, he once ranked his own multifarious talents in the order of calligraphy first, poetry second, prose third, and painting last. In saying this, he did not mention his extraordinary swordsmanship and his musical talent, nor his remarkable achievements as a playwright and drama critic. His Four Ape Cries, *a set of four plays ingeniously structured and brilliant in style, has been acknowledged as among the best of Ming drama. Ironically, though, Hsü has since been best known in Chinese art history, under his cognomen Master of the Green Vines Studio, an area he himself ranked last among his achievements. Cheng Hsieh*

(1693–1765), one of the Eight Eccentrics of Yangchow, made a seal for himself with the emblem "A Running Dog at the Threshold of the Green Vines." An echo of such worship was heard from Ch'i Pai-shih (1863–1957), one of China's greatest painters of the twentieth century, who once claimed that he would willingly serve as a slave in the household of the "Green Vines" in the next incarnation of his life. A vivid account of Hsü's life is provided in Yüan Hung-tao's "A Biography of Hsü Wen-ch'ang" in this anthology.

To Ma Ts'e-chih

My hair is white, my teeth are shaking, and yet I still hold an inch-long writing brush in hand, travel thousands of miles, and keep myself busy on a cold brick bed.[1] How is this in any way different from an old farm bull, with tears in his eyes and scabs all over his shoulders, who staggers along tilling in the fields and finds it hard to pull the plough anymore? Alas, how deplorable! Every time the season for water chestnuts and bamboo shoots arrives,[2] I am sure to sit quietly alone, in a trance, and what I miss most of all is where Ts'e-chih lives! Please take good care of my books in the cases; when I return, if my health permits, I'll read them with you.

Foreword to Yeh Tzu-shu's Poetry

A human being who has learned the speech of birds may sound like a bird but is by nature a human being. A bird who mimics human speech may sound like a human being but is by nature still a bird. This should surely be the standard by which to tell human beings from birds!

Those who write poetry today—are they any different from that? Having nothing to say themselves, they just steal what has already been said by others. They make the observation that a certain poem is after the style of such and such a person, and another one is not; that a certain line resembles the work of such and such a person, and another one does not. No matter how extremely skillful and how strikingly similar [to someone else's] such poetry is, it is no more than a bird mimicking human speech.

Now, my friend Tzu-shu's poems are not like that. He is honest and straightforward in personality; therefore, what he says is never obscure. He is interested in a wide variety of things and he is erudite; therefore, what he says knows no restrictions. He is by nature cheerful most of the time and seldom sad; therefore, what he says, even when bitter, can provide an emotional outlet. He aspires to the lofty-minded and disdains the ignoble; therefore, what he says, though terse, is actually rich in content. This is what I would call the kind of poetry that finds everything out of one's own mind and doesn't steal what has already been said by others. To discuss what he sings on his own based upon what he has learned by himself, to give advice against his slight blemishes so as to attain the utmost purity— these are what I could contribute to Tzu-shu. But to claim that a certain piece is not after such and such a style, that a certain line does not resemble that of such and such a person—it is surely not the way of someone who knows Tzu-shu well!

Another Colophon (On the Model Script "The Seventeenth" in the Collection of Minister Chu of the Court of the Imperial Stud)

Yesterday, on a visit to someone's garden, I saw some rare flowers embroidering its ground and some uncommon fruit trees reaching for the sky, but those were mixed with wild vines and prickly trailing plants. I looked back at my host and said, "How could you have given so much room to these guys?" The host said, "Indeed. But if they are all cast out, it won't make a garden."

I am not good at calligraphy, yet His Excellency Chu told me to write in the space at the beginning and end of this model script. Isn't his intention quite close to the remark of that host?

A Dream

I went deep into the mountains. It was smooth and effortless all the way. It was daytime. The broad road, tens of steps wide, was unpaved. Then I came to an undulating hill, at the northern foot of which there were four or five government office buildings, all facing south, with their doors closed, and with tens of soldiers on guard. Some strange birds and animals, each three or four in number, were tied up on the left side; I couldn't tell what they were. I walked up among these. The ground beneath suddenly quaked, and the buildings almost collapsed. I looked up north of the hill and saw the green pines there, lush like a kingfisher's feathers, and I ran fast until I came to a Taoist temple. I went in. The doorman took me to the master of the temple, who wore a yellow cap and a cotton gown. The doorman wanted me to stay there, but the master said, "This is not a place for you to stay." I was about to take leave when the master took out a notebook. He opened it and showed it to me, saying, "Your name is not Wei. The character 'Shen'[1] here—*that* is your name." The temple was extremely desolate, and both the doorman and the master wore shabby clothes.

Li Chih (1527–1602)

Li Chih, following in the footsteps of Wang Shou-jen, was one of the most individualistic thinkers of the Ming dynasty. A native of southern Fukien, Li won his degree of Provincial Graduate in 1552, but due to straitened circumstances did not participate in the metropolitan examination. After serving as an educational official in Honan for a while, he joined the faculty of the National University in Nanking and after a few years obtained a similar position in Peking. His subsequent appointments included junior positions in the Ministry of Rites in Peking and the Ministry of Justice in Nanking. In 1578 he assumed the post of prefect of Yao-an in the southwestern frontier province of Yunnan. During a three-year term of service there, just as during his previous assignments, Li had increasing difficulties getting along with his superiors and senior colleagues. In 1581 he resigned from his job and, at the age of fifty, decided to lead a commoner's life. The decision was probably made from frustration with his ever- worsening relationship with the authorities or from the realization that, without the degree of Metropolitan Graduate, he could never expect to get any significant official appointment.

He earned a living by private tutoring, and in 1585 he sent his family back to Fukien and went to live alone by a small lake named Dragon Pool outside the city of Ma-ch'eng in Hu-kuang, where he gave lectures on philosophy and society that attracted an intellectual audience. He devoted himself to writing and took breaks making visits to friends in adjacent counties. He spent most of his time avidly reading not only Confucian, Buddhist, and Taoist classics, but also novels and plays, which had generally been considered lowbrow literature. His marginal commentaries on the novel Water Margin (Shui-hu chuan) and the play The Western Chamber (Hsi-hsiang chi), revolutionary at the time, are still valuable for students of traditional Chinese fiction and drama today. During the last decade of the sixteenth century, Li made the acquaintance of the Yüan brothers, who visited him at Dragon Pool in 1593 and became his great admirers.

While Li Chih did cultivate a circle of admirers and friends among local officials, *who took turns inviting him over as a houseguest, he also became notorious to others for his nonconformist, unorthodox, and frequently iconoclastic behavior and speeches. Eventually this got him into trouble, and he was impeached and arrested in 1602. One day while in prison, he asked for a barber and found an opportunity to slash his throat with the latter's razor. On being asked why he tried to kill himself, his last words were, "What more does an old man of seventy want?"*

Li Chih enjoyed the relatively liberal cultural ambience of the late sixteenth century and became an eccentric in the convention of the Seven Sages of the Bamboo Grove of the Chin dynasty. He was an anachronism in the sense that much of his thought, especially that related to the reexamination and reevaluation of Confucianism, was far ahead of that of his contemporaries, perhaps by some three centuries. His posthumous influence was limited due to continual censorship and prohibition of his works throughout the Manchu dynasty. Li did exercise considerable influence on late Ming literature, primarily by providing a source of inspiration for the Yüan brothers. His famous essay on the importance of a "child's mind" provided the raison d'être for the emergence of a literary genre like the hsiao-p'in, *which emphasized casualness, originality, and spontaneity. As our selections here show, Li also wrote vignettes with a subtle irony or biting satire that Chang Tai compared to "arrows" and "daggers." Chung-tao, the youngest of the Yüan brothers, wrote a lively biography of Li Chih, which unfortunately is too lengthy to be included here.*

Three Fools

Liu I, an outspoken person, was inclined to reprimand others. Li Pai-yao[1] once told someone, "Although Liu I often reproved people, they didn't hate him." Aha! Someone like Pai-yao was indeed an understanding friend of Liu I's! I also have a tendency to reprimand people, yet people have not hated me. Why? It's because although I have a foul mouth, I am in fact warmhearted. Although my words are reviling, my intention is nevertheless good. I am warmhearted because I want people to improve themselves as quickly as possible. My intention is good because I always worry that people are not in a hurry to improve themselves. Therefore people who know me do not hate me.

However, although people in the world do not hate me, they do not befriend me either. There is only one guy who manages not only not to hate me, but also to befriend me, and that's Yang Ting-chien. Why is he able not to hate me and also befriend me? It's because I love rank and wealth, so I also love those who seek rank and wealth. If one loves rank, one has to study. Ting-chien, however, won't bring himself to study; therefore I reprove him. If one loves wealth, one has to save. Ting-chien cannot live within his income; therefore I reprove him. To reprove someone for not seeking rank and wealth—what is there to hate me for? On the other hand, there is indeed something about Ting-chien that deserves a scolding. When I was in dire straits at O-ch'eng, Ting-chien came to see me three or four times during the year, in spite of the summer heat and winter snow. There is something in his personal integrity that is above that of others. I know he is able to accomplish something—therefore, I constantly berate him. And yet there is no way that he can ever be changed, and I don't know why. He doesn't read. He's not eager to learn. He doesn't seek profit in the world. He doesn't seek social success. He has integrity, but no lofty ambition. So he is a fool after all and is not worthy of discussion.

Although Sheng-yu has some intention to achieve the Tao, he is not one who can go directly after it. He often sticks to dead, hackneyed words. He regards the hard work of everyday life as shackles and considers indulgence in rank and wealth the key to peace, happiness, and comfort. Consequently he cannot stay free from misleading others as well as misleading himself.

Ting-chien has personal integrity, but is not smart enough. Sheng-yu is smarter, but has no personal integrity. Both are fools in the mountains. Now that I am already in the company of such fools, I have no choice but to take things as they are for the rest of my life. And yet I cannot help chiding and railing at them all the time. So Ting-chien is a fool, Sheng-yu is a fool, and I myself am just another fool. Are we not three fools together? I hereby have written this note on the Three Fools.

In Praise of Liu Hsieh

Once there was a "learner of the Tao" who wore high-soled clogs or large-sized shoes, long sleeves and a broad belt, the cap of "cardinal guides and constant virtues," and the clothes of "human relationship."[1] He gleaned one- or two-tenths of what had been written, stole three- or four-tenths of what had been said, and claimed to be a true disciple of Chung-ni [Confucius].[2]

One day he ran into Liu Hsieh.[3] Now Liu Hsieh was a very smart scholar. When he saw the man, Liu ridiculed him: "You don't really understand my elder brother Chung-ni." Infuriated, the man stood up and said, "'If Heaven had not given birth to Chung-ni, it would have been a long, dark night through a myriad ages.'[4] Now who are you, and how dare you address him as Chung-ni and claim that he's your elder brother?" Liu Hsieh replied, "No wonder all the sages before the time of Hsi-huang[5] had to walk all day long holding paper flambeaux in their hands!" The man quietly took his leave.

Having heard about it, Mr. Li observed in approval, "What he said was brief and appropriate, terse and sapid, truly capable of clearing up all uncertainties and illuminating the world! From his words one may know what a man he is. Though an offhand bantering remark, the truth in it will remain unalterable for a hundred generations to come!"

A Lament for the Passing

If there is day, there is night. Similarly, if there is life, there is death. If something has passed away, it will never return. By the same token, if one has died, one cannot be alive again. All human beings want to live, but no one can live forever; all human beings mourn for what has passed away, but no one can stop it from passing away. Since one cannot live forever, one should give up the desire for [immortal] life. Since one cannot stop things from passing away, one should not mourn for what has passed away. I hereby make the following observation: Don't mourn for the dead; only the living deserve to be mourned. Don't mourn for what has passed away; better mourn for the living.

Inscription on a Portrait of Confucius at the Iris Buddhist Shrine

Everyone regards Confucius as a great sage, so I, too, regard him as a great sage. Everyone regards Taoism and Buddhism as heresies, so I, too, regard them as heresies. It is not that everyone really knows who a great sage is and what a heresy is; it is only because everyone has heard so much of it from the instruction of his father and his teacher. It is not that his father and his teacher really know who a great sage is and what a heresy is; it is only because they have heard so much of it from the teachings of previous Confucians. It is not that previous Confucians really knew who a great sage was and what a heresy was; it is only because Confucius himself had made observations on the issue. When he said, "I am not good enough to be a saint," it was out of his modesty. When he said, "Attack heresies," he was surely referring to Taoism and Buddhism.

Previous Confucians made their remarks on assumption, fathers and teachers echo and recite those remarks, and pupils simply listen to them as if they were blind and deaf themselves. When ten thousand people say something in one voice, it becomes irrefutable. When something has remained unchanged for a thousand years, a person doesn't understand it by himself any more. He won't quote, "I'm merely reciting his words." Instead he'll quote, "I already know the man." He won't quote, "Pretend to know what one doesn't know." Instead he'll only quote, "I claim to know something when I do know it." By now, even when a person does have eyes, he'll have no use for them anymore.[1]

Now who am I? How dare I claim to have eyes of my own? All I have to do is follow the general trend. Since I have followed the general trend in regarding Confucius as a sage and followed the general trend in worshipping him, therefore I will still follow the general trend in worshipping him here at the Iris Buddhist Shrine.[2]

Essay: On the Mind of a Child

Toward the end of his commentary on *The Western Chamber*,[1] the Mountain Farmer of Dragon Cave[2] observed, "I hope those who understand me won't think that I still have the mind of a child." Now, the mind of a child is the true mind. If a child's mind is to be dismissed, then the true mind is dismissed. The mind of a child, being the natural mind at its initial stage, is purely innocent and free from falseness. If the mind of a child is lost, the true mind is lost. If the true mind is lost, then the true person is lost. To be a person who is not true is to lose all origin.

A child is the beginning of a person. The mind of a child is the beginning of a mind. How can one afford to lose the beginning of a mind? Now, how does one suddenly lose the mind of a child? It is because at the beginning stage, some information enters the mind through the ears and the eyes; when it is allowed to dominate inside, the mind of a child is lost. As one grows up, some reasoning enters the mind from the information, and when it is allowed to dominate inside, the mind of a child is lost. By and by, with the daily increase in reasoning and information, one knows and feels more each day. When one knows that a good reputation is something desirable, and when one tries one's best to attain that, the mind of a child is lost. When one knows that a bad reputation is something undesirable, and when one tries one's best to avoid it, the mind of a child is lost. Now, all reasoning and information comes from extensive reading and moral reasoning, and who among the ancient sages didn't read? But, even when they didn't read, they would still keep their mind of a child, and even when they did read a lot, they would protect and preserve their mind of a child, unlike scholars today, who have blocked up their child's mind with extensive reading and moral reasoning. Since our scholars have blocked up their child's mind with extensive reading and moral reasoning, then why did the sages expound their ideas in writing, thus keeping our scholars benighted? Once the mind of a child is blocked up, when they say something, what they say is insincere. When they do something in their administrative affairs, what they do becomes groundless. And when they write something, what they write makes no sense. It has no depth, no grace, no substance, and no illumination. Not a single word of virtue may be found therein. Why is it so? It is only because the mind of a child has been blocked up, and information and reasoning that come from outside have taken its place inside.

Now, when information and reasoning dominate the mind, then when one speaks, it is from that information and reasoning, not from the mind of a child itself. Even when the saying is artful, what's the good to me? Isn't it a false person saying false words, doing false things, and writing false compositions? When a person is false, then everything he does is false. Accordingly, if one says false words to false people, they will be pleased; if one talks about false things to false people, they will be pleased; if one discusses false compositions with false people, they will be pleased. If everything one does is false, then everyone one talks to is pleased. When the entire theater is false, how can a short person make any distinction?[3] Hence, although the very best of writings do exist in the world, there must have been much that sank into oblivion among short people, never to be read by later generations! Why? It is because all the world's very best writings originate from the mind of a child. If the mind of a child is always preserved, then all that information and reasoning will never take its place, and there will be great literature in every age, from every person, and in every creative and original form and style. In the case of poetry, why must it be like *The Old Poems* [Ku shih] and *The Anthology* [Wen hsüan]?[4] In the case of prose, why must it be like the pre-Ch'in?[5] So it was passed down to the Six Dynasties, and it changed into the new forms;[6] then it changed successively into the romance [ch'uan-ch'i]),[7] the promptbook [*yüan-pen*],[8] the miscellaneous play [*tsa-chü*],[9] *The Western Chamber* and *Water Margin*,[10] and the examination essays of today. Past or present, as long as it is a great sage talking about the "way of the sages," it is excellent writing, and one should not judge by priority in temporal order. From this, I have therefore come to the conclusion that all that comes from the mind of a child is excellent writing by itself. Why should one talk about the Six Classics,[11] *The Analects*, and *Mencius* only?

With respect to the Six Classics, *The Analects*, and *Mencius*, they were either overestimated by official historians or praised excessively by officials —or by those pedantic disciples or ignorant pupils, recalling what their teachers had said. Sometimes they got the beginning but lost the conclusion. Sometimes they remembered the later part but missed the earlier sayings. Or they just put down whatever they perceived. Latecomers didn't know the truth, so they regarded those [words] as having come out of the mouths of the sages themselves and decided to canonize them as classics. Who ever realized that many were not the sayings of the sages themselves? Even if they were indeed from the sages themselves, they were meant for specific occasions, nothing more than making offhand prescriptions and passing out medicine according to the illness, so as to rescue those ignorant pupils and pedantic disciples. It was difficult to cure the illness of falsehood with set prescriptions. How could it be regarded as the ultimate truth, which applies to all ages? Therefore the Six Classics, *The Analects*, and *Mencius* have become a pretext for those "learners of the Tao" and a haven for all hypocrites, and should never be considered as equal to expressions of the mind of a child. Alas! How can I ever have a chance to discuss writings with a truly great sage who has not lost his mind of a child?

T'u Lung (1542–1605)

A native of Yin-hsien County (Ning-po in modern times), Chekiang, T'u Lung won the degree of Metropolitan Graduate in 1577. After serving a short term as a magistrate elsewhere, T'u became the magistrate of the populous and scenic Ch'ing-p'u County east of Soochow, where he enjoyed himself among the beautiful lakes and hills of the region and held frequent drinking and poetry-composing parties with local literati. One who attended such parties was Wang Shih-chen, the most eminent literary figure of the century, who regarded T'u as a literary ally and later ranked him as one of the Last Five Masters. It was also during his service in Ch'ing-p'u that T'u started his serious lifelong study of Taoism as a religion. T'u never neglected his official business, though, and became very popular with local people. He was promoted to the rank of director in the Ministry of Rites in Peking, but before long was dismissed from office after being indicted by a personal enemy. When he passed by Ch'ing-p'u on his way home, local residents tried to persuade him to stay by offering him land and property, but he declined and left after having attended drinking parties for three days.

Back at home, T'u spent most of his time drinking and writing poetry with his friends, and made a living writing tomb inscriptions and other commemorative prose pieces on commission. Sometimes he composed by dictation while playing chess with a friend, and he was always ahead of the recorder. Both his daughter and daughter-in-law were good poets, and they often wrote in response to his compositions.

T'u respected Wang Shih-chen as a mentor and was an eloquent neoclassicist critic in the latter's camp. Unlike Wang, though, T'u was not entirely unsympathetic to the views of the Kung-an school led by the Yüan brothers. T'u was also an accomplished dramatist: three of his plays, including one that had as its protagonist the great T'ang poet Li Po, are still available today. Lin Yutang translated into English T'u's travel notes, The Travels of Mingliaotse, *but it has long been out of print and available only in a few university libraries. His prose has been admired for its exquisite diction and resonant lyricism.*

A Letter in Reply to Li Wei-yin

My office in the executive mansion, where incense is being burned, is like the abode of a Buddhist monk. With a pot of spring water and a volume of an alchemist's manual, every day I engage in thoughts beyond this dusty world. As regards the documents and files of the Orchid Department,[1] they are taken care of by the section chiefs, who hardly ever submit any report, and it has turned out that I have become a gentleman of leisure keeping company with clouds and waters.

There is nothing I fear more than going out on the back of an ambling horse, grabbing a horsewhip as if holding something prickly, and pushing my way in the whirling wind that sends flying sand into my face. At such times, I meditate on the blue streams and emerald rocks in Chiang-nan to cheer myself up. I do have the whirling wind and the flying sand in my face, but I also have the blue streams and emerald rocks in my mind, so what's the harm? Every time I am on horseback in the grand company of a thousand horsemen, with the dust flying all around me, I, your humble servant, carefree and at ease, raise my head to look at the clouds and the sky, and let my mind soar into the vast. While pacing to and fro, I compose a poem in an instant.

At the fifth beat of the night watches I report to the court. My robe is veiled in the cool, refreshing mist. The moon shines over the trees in the palace. Dismounting from horseback, I walk on the imperial carriageway and cross the palace moat. My mind travels far into the mountains where immortals reside and indulges in the art of singing about irises. While my body is clothed in official robes, my heart is in the misty ravines. People around me, who see what I look like but do not know my mind, take me as just another courtier. The beauty and wonder of land and water in Chiang-nan find their embodiment in what I have noted down while standing by the left side-gate of the palace.

My honorable friend, you live by the ferry along the Ch'in-huai River,[2] where the moon shines after the mist vanishes, where the waters are green and the clouds rosy at sunrise and sunset, thousands of miles away from the land of wind and sands, and yet you sound so dejected and ill at ease in your letter. Why? In general, a man of learning should value accommodating his mind to the surroundings, not accommodating the surroundings to his mind. If the mind is at peace, all the dust will settle down in the Clear Void.[3]

If our inmost heart is in chaos, even in quiet seclusion troubles will arise in all and sundry ways. My honorable friend, do you agree with me or not?

Tsou Yüan-piao[4] said something in court that offended our Sagacious Sovereign,[5] so he had to leave again for Mo-ling.[6] He is an honest, uncorrupted, and straightforward man, a great asset to the state. Now you may enjoy his company day and night.

It is a fine morning. Over the fragrant meadow, the spring wind from the northeast wafts gently. But, looking southward to where you are, my "beautiful one,"[7] how my heart aches!

To a Friend, while Staying in the Capital

In the city of Yen[1] one wears a hood to cover the face and rides a yellow horse. When the wind arises, flying dust is all over the streets and alleys. When one alights from horseback on coming home, one's nostrils become as black as a chimney. The excrement of people and horses is mixed with dirt and sand. After a rain, the mire is up to one's horse-saddle and knees. Commoners, whipping their hobbling donkeys, race with one another to shoulder their way along with officeholders. When the way is being cleared for a high-ranking official to pass, they all run in a hurry, trying to take cover in a winding lane in time. One quickly becomes short of breath after running like crazy, and one's sweat flows all the way down to one's heels. Such is the taste of life up here.

My mind goes far away to a riverside village in the setting sun, to a fishing boat on its way back to the cove, to the lingering sunlight that penetrates into the woods, to sands bright like snow, to a fishnet hung out to dry under the flowers, to the white signboard and azure flag of a tavern looming from behind drooping willows, to an old man walking out of his fagot gate with fish and wine jug in hand. To take a stroll on the sands with a couple of good friends—it is far superior to rushing on horseback into the mud of Ch'ang-an.[2]

To a Friend, after Coming Home in Retirement

Once passing through the Gate of Splendor,[1] I've been in a different world away from Ch'ang-an. Lying down by night, I've never had a single dream about the clatter of a horse's hooves around the Hua-ch'ing Palace.[2]

Back at home here, I have my Iris-Picking Hall. Behind the hall, there are three storied buildings with small trees and bamboos planted around them. Both the bedroom and the kitchen are in the shade of the bamboos. Resting on my pillow I often listen to the singing of birds. To the west of the house there are two old cassia trees, more than a hundred years of age. When they blossom in autumn, the whole courtyard is filled with fragrance. I've found some space to dig out a small pond, and have planted some pink and white lotus flowers in it. By the side of the pond there are a few peach trees. In the third [lunar] month the pink brocade of their bloom finds its reflection on the water, like thousands of beautiful women mirroring themselves in the waters of O-p'ang Palace or the labyrinth of Mi-lou.[3] There are also hibiscus and knotweed flowers, which enhance the melancholy grace in autumn. What is even more pleasant is that people in the streets here, though they are extremely poor, do not put on airs by aping the extravagance and pomp of the gentry houses in the regions of Wu and Yüeh.[4]

Ch'en Chi-ju (1558–1639)

Known as a child prodigy, Ch'en Chi-ju made a name for himself equal to that of his close friend Tung Ch'i-ch'ang (1555–1636) while both of them were students at the prefectural school. However, they took different roads in the jungle of the world in their later careers. Tung went up the social ladder until he was appointed a cabinet minister and became the most famous and important calligrapher and painter of the age. Ch'en gave up his political career at the age of twenty-eight, with the memorable expressionist act of burning all his scholar's caps and gowns, and went to lead a commoner's life in the beautiful lakes and hills of Sung-chiang Prefecture, Southern Metropolitan Region, his native land. Nevertheless, his fame as a versatile and erudite scholar, poet, and painter spread far and wide. Cabinet ministers and governors took pride in inviting Mei-kung (Ch'en's cognomen, lit., "Master Brow") to be their houseguest or in visiting him. Tung Ch'i-ch'ang even had a storied building constructed at his own villa specifically named for Ch'en's occasional visits.

Besides his artistic and literary pursuits in many different fields, Ch'en was acknowledged as an arbiter of fashion in all kinds of epicurean pleasures, from floriculture and landscape architecture to gastronomy. His enjoyment of close contacts with his prestigious and powerful friends won him the reputation of being the "Grand Councillor in the Mountains," in spite of his alleged reclusion. This perhaps accounts for the posthumous accusation of hypocrisy and dilettantism represented by a satirical poem written by the renowned Ch'ing poet and playwright Chiang Shih-ch'üan (1725–85) with the lines "Lightly the crane in the cloud flies / In and out of the houses of prime ministers." Ch'en did decline, on the excuse of ill health, numerous official appointments resulting from recommendations to the throne from his friends in court, probably out of his determination to stay away from the political intrigues and partisanship of the Wan-li reign. However, he was honored in various literary circles. Although he was himself a protégé of Wang Shih-chen's, Ch'en also befriended the Yüan brothers and Chung Hsing, thus providing a liaison between the old and the new camps. He enjoyed a long and rich life, and at his death left a meticulously detailed will for his family.

Quite a few passages from Ch'en's books of random notes are available in English in Lin Yutang's superb translation, contained in his anthology The Importance of Understanding, *but our selection does not overlap those. Ch'en's vignettes shine with wit and humor and flow with carefree ease.*

Trips to See Peach in Bloom

There is a lot of sunshine at the southern city wall. Beneath it there lies a host of peach trees, the flowers of which flourish with the sunlight and the water. Local residents have planted slender elms and gentle willows, which form hedges and fences. Vegetable plots and flower gardens are interwoven into one another like embroidery.

One day after the Birthday of the Flowers,[1] I summoned the mountain recluse Ch'en and his son and asked them to warm up some wine and bring it along with a small carrying case of food. In the company of Hu An-fu, Sung Pin-chih, and Meng Chih-fu, we crossed the bridge and walked to the east of the city wall, where some peach trees were bursting into bloom.

We pushed open the gate and stormed in [to a garden]. An old man was feasting his guests. We rushed to the table to beg for wine and asked him to have the table moved under the flowering branches. The old man looked at us in astonishment, but he followed our instructions respectfully. Without telling him our names, we played gluttons in wining and dining at his table. Then we climbed up the branch of a peach tree, sat among flowers, and played the game of fist-hiding. Winners and losers got up and down in turn. The five or six of us made a living windlass in the red rain.[2] Or we could be likened to lonely apes or crazy birds poking among leaves and looking for fruit. Our only worry was that the branch might be too brittle to carry our weight! We didn't disband until dusk. On that day, the old man was having a birthday party concurrently with the celebration of the Birthday of the Flowers. After a couple of drinks I composed a song and presented it to the old man, in which I proposed that he provide food and wine to hold another birthday celebration the next day.

On the fourteenth, Hsi-chou, Chih-fu, Shu-yi, and I set out carrying wine and food cases. As soon as we came to the road that led out of the city gate, we ran into Po-ling and Tzu-yu and dragged them along. Then we also met Administrator Yüan,[3] who was entering the city wearing a cape made of crane feathers. Hearing that we were making a trip to look at the flowers, the administrator turned back and went to Peach Blossom Brook with us.

When we arrived, Mr. T'ien was weeding with a hoe.[4] Seeing us, he went inside to change clothes and then came out to invite us in. The guests scattered around and squatted on rocks. An-fu, Pin-chih, Ch'i-chung, and his son all brought food cases and wine for the occasion. Catching a glimpse of us from atop the city wall, the three gentlemen—Tung, Hsü, and Ho—got excited and staggered down, bringing with them wine, fresh bamboo shoots, and clams for the company. At that time there were eighteen of us who assembled without previous arrangement. Counting Mr. T'ien's son Kuei-p'ien, there were nineteen. Altogether there were eleven food cases and seven or eight jugs of wine. The wine was finished, but we had just reached the height of our enthusiasm. The flowers might have got drunk, yet we remained unintoxicated. We were just about to start feeling frustrated with the empty bottles and jugs, when a jar of wine was hauled down to us by means of a long rope from above the city wall. The newcomers were the brothers Wen-ch'ing and Chih-ch'ing. We were overjoyed and acclaimed them as men of refined taste.

Now people formed into groups, and each group played its own game. The administrator and Po-ling were fighting a battle of wits at the table, and all those guys present were suffering from their empty fists.[5] The host, short-haired and with long ears, talked and laughed in dotage. Seeing that there was still a little wine left, we stopped whoever happened to pass by outside the flowered hedges and, without considering whether it was an acquaintance or a stranger, whether he was good-looking or unattractive, we just poured a cup of wine down his throat and stuck a twig of peach flower in his hair by the temple; everyone left in great delight, believing this to be auspicious. When the sun had set and the birds had become weary, we also went back. We leaned on one another for support beneath the moon. Our gauze hoods and silk sleeves were mostly covered with wine stains and flower petals.

In the past, T'ao, the Gentleman Summoned to Office, wrote his own mind in telling us how the residents of the Peach Blossom Spring had fled from the upheavals during the Ch'in. He used the place as a fable; actually there was no such place as Peach Blossom Spring. Now the peach flowers here are so close to the city wall, but no one wrote about the flowers and made them known to those who might be interested. But, after I "inquired about the ferry," within a few days a footpath has taken shape beneath the flowers. Except for men like us, how many would really appreciate and protect those flowers? On the other hand, several people have crushed the flowers like a furious wind or a torrential rain, turning the rosy cloud into a miserable mess. Then, with such a criminal case of damaging the peach flowers, this humble fellow here is half-commendable and half-guilty.[6]

Inscription on Wang Chung-tsun's
A History of Flowers

My farmhouse is located among crisscrossing waters. Besides a few kinds of flowers, I keep only some earthen pots, a bamboo couch, and books of the Three Schools.[1] All these are useless things except to people who have perceived the Tao. I do have a mania for flowers, though. Around the two equinoxes, every day I direct my low-capped and long-bearded servants[2] to move or plant my flowers, exposing myself to wind and dew and forgetting to comb my hair or take a bath. A visitor quipped, "Our Brow Taoist has the peach flower in his destiny."[3] I retorted, "It is a flower along with the Post-Horse Star."[4]

Having little to do in seclusion, I once thought about working on a history of flowers to be handed down to my children and grandchildren, and did not expect that my friend Wang Chung-tsun would get ahead of me. *A History of Flowers*, a work by him in twenty-four sections, consists of interesting anecdotes about people of old times. It should have a place in the future along with books about farming and horticulture. Those who have read this book, if they manage to age among flowers, may live a long life in this world; if they learn the rules and principles to break through brambles and sweep away gravel, to irrigate and to cultivate, they may make use of those to govern in the world; if they decline the positions of minister and chamberlain and engage themselves in "watering the garden,"[5] then they may create for themselves a refuge away from the world, or live in defiance of the world. But those who fly and eat meat[6] may not be able to appreciate it.

A Colophon to *A History of Flowers*

Those who have access to rural pleasures but do not know how to enjoy them are woodcutters and herdsmen. Those who have access to fruit and melons but have no time to savor them are greengrocers and peddlers. Those who have access to flowers and trees but are unable to appreciate them are men of rank and wealth.

Among the worthies of the old times, Yüan-ming was the only one who frequently found his pleasure among mulberry, flax, pines, and chrysanthemums, and between the fields or by the hedges. T'ung-p'o was fond of planting and was able to tend flowers and trees all by himself. It is something inherent in one's nature, not to be imposed. If we try to force it on someone, even if we present to him *A History of Flowers*, he would angrily throw it away and take his leave. If it is really something close to your nature, and you are really fond of it, then please pick up the book, lie down in the sun by the woods, and watch carefully how the flowers bloom and fall. In that case, how is it in any way different from tracing the rise and decline of dynasties over tens of thousands of years? We may even claim that all of the twenty-one histories are contained in this one unofficial history.[1]

A Colophon to *A Profile of Yao P'ing-chung*

Without an understanding of the Tao, how could one ever get through the Passes of the Four Words—Life, Age, Illness, and Death? There is nothing more pathetic than the aging and illness of beautiful women and celebrated generals, as in the cases of Lady Li and General Ma.[1] When rosy cheeks are replaced by white hairs, when a tigerlike, gallant young warrior turns into an old man with wrinkled skin, what pleasure is there any more? Hsi-tzu went to the Five Lakes.[2] Yao P'ing-chung entered the Blue Castle Mountains. It was unlikely that they would escape death in a number of years, but at least the ugly last stage of their life was not to be seen by others. Hence the saying, "A divine dragon shows its head to people, but not its tail."[3]

Selections from *Privacies in the Mountains*

1

During the five beats of the night watch,[1] the birds in the mountains startle and make noises five times. It is known as the "night beat alarm" and in fact becomes a substitute for the clepsydra and sandglass in the mountains. I remember that once, when I lived at the foot of the Smaller Mount K'un-shan,[2] it had just cleared up after the plum rain[3] and my guests were draining their wine bowls. Then I happened to hear the frogs croaking in the courtyard and alerted my guests to listen to the sound and regulate their drinking. I composed an antithetical couplet:

> Flowering branches wave the guests farewell;
> Frogs beat time on their drums.
> Rustling bamboos resound in the forest;
> Birds keep up the night watch.

First-hand observations of life in the mountains, indeed!

2

In an empty valley, you're just awake, and you hear the footsteps of friends coming. You contemplate joining them for an exploration of the pine and cassia through cloud and mist, when some gentlemen who take pride in their own talents always insist on picking a title and assigning the rhyme-scheme words, and then lavish enormous pains on composing and chanting. For a quiet man, to cope with that situation is really like a clear stream struggling to free itself of fallen leaves, or a deep forest sizzling with the raucous sound of droning cicadas. That is why it has been said that in the absence of a poet, a company may spare itself the trouble of accumulating several scores of poems composed as responses to one another, which is no small matter, really!

3

Flowers to be kept in vases and placed on the table each have their own proper place. The fragrant early plum [*Prunus mume*],[1] which stands proudly in the snow, always stays around a versifying soul.[2] The apricot, which charms in spring, is most lovely by a dressing mirror. Pear blossoms, which weep in the rain, will break a maiden's heart in her boudoir. The lotus, which braves the wind, will invite a grin on rosy cheeks. The crab apple, the peach, and the plum [*Prunus salicina*] vie with one another in glamour at a sumptuous banquet. The peony makes the best ornament for the fan of a singing girl. A twig of fragrant cassia will suffice to start a pleasant conversation. A bouquet of quiet orchids will make a proper keepsake for the dear departed. By the same token, you set each kind in its proper ambience, and there will usually be agreement between scene and mood.

4

Most of the ancient hermits devoted themselves to tilling in the fields; but I am frail and feeble, so that's the first thing I'm unable to do. Most of them took up hunting and fishing; but I refrain from killing, so that's the second thing I'm unable to do. Most of them owned some thirty acres of land and about eight hundred mulberry trees;[1] but I am poor and indigent, so that's the third thing I'm unable to do. Most of them were able to subsist on water and meals of thin gruel; but I cannot stand hardship and hunger, so that's the fourth thing I'm unable to do. The only thing I am able to do is to live quietly on plain fare and engage myself in writing. To be a writer, however, make sure never to criticize sages of the past. You may enumerate what one is right about, but do not make it a business to prove what others are wrong in.

5

When seafood is not salty, when preserved fruit is not sweet, when a man of letters who has retired from the world is not arrogant, and when an eminent Buddhist monk does not prattle about Zen, they demonstrate the ultimate virtue.

6

A celebrated courtesan leafing through scriptures, an old Buddhist monk brewing wine, a military general indulging himself in the garden of literary imagination, a scholar charging onto a battlefield—they may have lost their respective original characters, but these are very tasteful things to do.

7

In the third month the bamboo shoots have just grown juicy, and the drowsy plum wind[1] has not yet begun. In the ninth month the water-shield and the perch are most sensational,[2] and the sorghum wine smells really good. This is the best time to sit by a sunny window with some nice friends, take out some ancient calligraphy masterworks or famous paintings, and appreciate and discuss them while some incense is burning in the room.

8

To live in the mountains, you need a small boat with crimson balustrades, blue roofing, bright windows, and a short sail. In the boat you place a miscellany of books, maps, and bronze vessels, as well as various kinds of wine, tea, preserved fruit, and dried meat. For a short trip, you may stop at the Peaks by Lake Mao.[1] For a long trip, you go no farther than Ching-k'ou in the north or Ch'ien-t'ang in the south.[2] When the wind is favorable and everything goes smoothly on the way, you may travel over to visit some old friends. If invited, you might as well stay for a chat overnight or for a drinking party for ten days. If you find some mountains and waters with a great view, or come upon the lodging of an eminent monk or a recluse, where luxuriant bamboos and trees are set off by grass and flowers, you may tie up your hair in a piece of silk, carry your walking cane, put on your sandals, and face them with composure. Sometimes, when the view is unspectacular but still refreshing, you play a note on your steel flute in the clear void of water and moonshine, and the white gulls seem about to start dancing. It is just another way to escape from the hubbub of the world and to avoid visitors.

Yüan Tsung-tao (1560–1600)

The three Yüan brothers were natives of Kung-an County in Hu-kuang Province (which later, in the Ch'ing dynasty, was divided into Hunan and Hupei Provinces) who put their hometown on the map of Chinese literary history by founding the Kung-an school. Tsung-tao, the eldest brother, an admirer of Po Chü-i (the T'ang poet) and Su Shih, named his studio after them. The collection of his literary works is titled Works from the Po-Su Studio. Unlike his idols, who lived long lives, Tsung-tao was only forty when he died. After having barely survived an unknown disease at the age of twenty, he devoted much of his time to reading Taoist scriptures and to the Taoist practice of deep breathing and meditation, and turned his attention to preparing for the civil service examinations only after his father's repeated demands. He won his Metropolitan Graduate degree with high honors in 1586. After various appointments in the imperial court he was appointed in 1597 as a private secretary of the heir apparent.

Taking advantage of the relative leisure of a courtier's life, Tsung-tao spent much of his time reading, gardening, and making trips to places with scenic views around the capital. At his premature death Tsung-tao was in such straitened circumstances that even the cost of his coffin and funeral had to be provided by his followers, and his wife and children had to sell his collection of calligraphy and paintings, desk, and inksticks to pay for their journey home.

Tsung-tao was also known as a calligrapher and painter and tried his hand at drama. Unfortunately, the manuscripts of the two plays he wrote are said to have been destroyed by mice. In terms of fame and influence he was eclipsed by his brother Hung-tao, but it was Tsung-tao who first stood up against the theory of the neoclassicist camp in his essay on prose writing and, as observed by Ch'ien Ch'ien-i, laid the foundation for the Kung-an school. His prose is graceful, poised, and pleasing in its search for new ways of expression and original figures of speech.

41

Little Western Paradise

As we turned west at Lu-kou Bridge,[1] all of a sudden the carriage bells and sooty dust were out of view. Along the road the indigos were in bloom, and the entire valley was a purplish blue. I felt like a bird just let out of a cage that, upon sudden sight of the grass and trees in the open field after days of confinement, imagines itself to be back at its old nest.

We stayed for the night at a rural temple. The halls were dilapidated and the beds shaky. Only the murals were somewhat worth seeing. We got up in the morning and moved on for some twenty to thirty miles. In front of us, lofty mountain peaks towered above the heads of our horses. We ascended along the crevice of a cliff. When we came atop the cliff all the peaks again loomed in front. Facing us, two pointed peaks soared like a pair of female breasts. One of the mountains stood upright, majestic and virile —that was the so-called Little Western Paradise.[2]

After this point, the road was not as rough. We rode along the foot of the mountain where [the vista] was wide above and narrow below, so it looked like we were moving in an arcade. It was getting dark by then, and we heard distant thunder. When we reached halfway up the mountain, we looked at one another and, worrying about a possible rainstorm approaching, dashed ahead until we reached the Eastern Valley Temple.

Outside the gate of the temple there was a grove of white poplar trees. The wind howled and wailed. Sleepless at night, I invited everyone to join me for a drink at an open expanse of land to the right side of the temple gate, where the ground was clean and smooth, like a place set apart for wheat-threshing. I proposed a game of wager. Each one of us took a turn telling a story about a ghost or a tiger, and it had to be an event within the last year or two, not anything already noted in books of the past. The one who couldn't do it would be penalized by having to drink up a huge *kung*.[3] A friend started telling a story about a tiger, but quickly gave up when he had barely begun. Everyone present rocked with laughter.

A Trip to Sukhāvatī Temple

The water under High Beam Bridge, which has its origin in the deep ravine of the Western Hills, now runs into the Jade River—a thousand bolts of white cloth. A breeze moves across its surface, making it look like ribbed tissue paper. The embankment stands in the water, tapped by ripples on both sides. There are four columns of green willows: the trees are old and the leaves lush. The shade of each tree is big enough to accommodate seats for several persons. The hanging threads are about twelve feet in length.

On the northern bank there are a multitude of Buddhist and Taoist temples, the crimson gates and sky-blue halls of which extend for tens of miles. The distant trees on the other side, varying in height, gather closely together, and paddy fields lie between them. The Western Hills, in the shape of conch shells like a woman's hair-buns, loom among the woods and the water.

Sukhāvatī Temple is about a mile away from the bridge.[1] The road leading up there is also spectacular. Our horses trot in the green shade as if under a huge umbrella. In front of the main hall there are a few pine trees, the trunks of which are mottled bright green and yellow like large fish scales. Their size is about seven or eight arm-spans around.

I once made a trip there on vacation, in the company of Huang Ssu-li and others. My younger brother Hung-tao said, "This place is not unlike the Su Embankment in Ch'ien-t'ang."[2] Ssu-li agreed. I sighed. The great view of West Lake had long been in my dreams. When would I be able to hang up my official cap, become a tourist under the Six Bridges, and settle my sentimental account with the hills and waters there? On that day, we each composed a poem on a different rhyme scheme before we disbanded.

A Trip to Yüeh-yang

Along the way from Stonehead to Yüeh-yang, the water was clear as a mirror and the hills were like conch shells.[1] I couldn't see enough of it from behind the awninged window on my boat. The most sensational view was at Inkstick Mountain. It had a circumference of only ten miles, and yet the boat traveled for two days, having covered some sixty to seventy miles, and we were still going round and round at the foot of the mountain. At dawn the sun rose from behind, and at dusk it set behind the same spot. Both the morning sunshine and the evening glow flooded the same area. That was because the river was winding through Inkstick Mountain, so the boat was also making its twists and turns inside the mountain. Although the boat was actually going rather fast, we somehow felt that it was extremely slow.

When we passed by Yüeh-yang we wanted to make a trip to Lake Tung-t'ing, but a stormwind kept us from going there. My youngest brother, Chung-tao, a Cultivated Talent,[2] composed a piece of prose, "A Curse on Liu the Cultivated Talent," which contained many gibes.[3] By early dusk the wind had turned ferocious, blowing up thundering waves. Near the shore the water was ruffled into a bed of white foam; the boat almost capsized. My youngest brother said, "Could it be Liu the Cultivated Talent seeking his revenge?" I said, smiling, "It is quite common for good friends to tease each other." We both laughed. The wind did not calm down until the next day.

Selections from *Miscellanea*

1

Sitting close to the stove, I suddenly heard a sound like "Tut! Tut!" Listening more carefully, I found it to be coming from the kettle. My servant-boy asked me, "What is that?" I said, "Such sound comes from the movement of earth, water, fire, and wind." The boy said, "When a man sighs, uttering 'Tut! Tut!' What makes him do that?" I said, "It is also from earth, water, fire, and wind. I, you, and the kettle—all three are the same!"

2

If you have not yet reached a comprehensive and thorough understanding of things in learning, then you are likely to say yes to those who agree with you, and say no to those who don't. It is like a southerner in a boat sneering at a northerner in a carriage,[1] or the long-legged crane spurning the short-legged duck.[2] Not to reprove yourself for holding a prejudice, but to reprove others for holding a different opinion—isn't that preposterous?

3

For farmers and artisans, merchants and peddlers, grooms and cooks, attendants and servants, what they are called upon to perform varies from day to day and month to month, and the way they speak also varies from day to day and month to month, because these are always new. Only in pursuing vulgar learning does one spend all one's life sucking the saliva of others, and not have a single new word to say. How despicable!

4

Someone asked me, "Now such and such two guys are of the same kind, so why is it that one of them is always happy and the other extremely miserable?" I said, "What is there in happiness that makes it superior to misery?" He said again, "What one receives and enjoys in happiness is entirely different from what another receives and enjoys in misery. How can they be the same?" I said, smiling, "What is there in receiving and enjoying that makes it superior to not receiving and not enjoying?" The man said angrily, "You are really dumb!" I said, "What is there in not being dumb that makes it superior to being dumb?" The man laughed and desisted.

5

Indeed there have been many men of letters who achieved great prestige and reputation, but none has ever surpassed Po Chü-i in that.[1] There is no need to talk about the high price [for his poems] in the Rooster Woods,[2] or the rise in status of singing girls [for being able to sing his poems]. Now in the streets of Ching-chou there is a certain Ko Tzu-ch'ing. A vulgar middleman, that's all! He has Po Chü-i's poems tattooed all over his body below the neck, and under every poem a picture is tattooed. There are more than thirty of these altogether. People call him "the walking picture of Secretary Po's poetry." How weird!

Yüan Hung-tao (1568–1610)

Hung-tao, the second and most influential of the Yüan brothers, who held the banner of the Kung-an school, displayed leadership talent when he was only fifteen, chairing a literary society at the county school that consisted of members who were old enough to be his father. Following in the footsteps of Tsung-tao, Hung-tao decided to abide by the prescribed order of his age and society; he studied hard and won his degree of Metropolitan Graduate in 1592. Instead of seeking an official appointment, Hung-tao went back home to spend more time with his family and friends, and traveled widely. The Yüan brothers met the unorthodox thinker Li Chih and were so fascinated by him that they called upon his Iris Buddhist Shrine at Dragon Pool in 1593 and stayed there for more than three months. Li Chih was also impressed with their talent, and they formed a "friendship oblivious of age difference" (wang nien chih chiao). After a few years Hung-tao was convinced by Li Chih, who saw in him not only talent but also personal integrity, to seek an official career. He served in many central and local government positions, including a directorship in the Ministry of Personnel.

After the death of Tsung-tao, Hung-tao took the lead in a verbal war against the neoclassicism of Wang Shih-chen and the Later Seven Masters and their retrogressive ideas of literary history. As leader of the Kung-an school, Hung-tao promoted individuality, spontaneity, and what he called "natural sensibility" (hsing ling). His extensive influence in the literary arena of the late Ming was achieved through his numerous writings in different genres and his large circle of friends and admirers. His hsiao-p'in compositions excel in their brisk tempo, youthful zest, and vivid description. Chang Tai placed Hung-tao's travel notes in the highest rank of the genre, praising them as second to none but those of Li Tao-yüan (the Northern Wei author of A Commentary on the Water Classic) and the T'ang prose master Liu Tsung-yüan.

Of the authors introduced in this collection, Yüan Hung-tao is better known in the West than most. Interested readers may explore Jonathan Chaves's superb

translation of poems and prose by the three brothers, and Chih-p'ing Chou's criti-
cal study of Yüan Hung-tao and the Kung-an school.

First Trip to West Lake

Going west out of the Wu-lin Gate, as soon as I saw the Paoshu Pagoda soaring among layers of cliffs ahead, my heart started leaping across the lake. By noon we entered the Celebration Temple,[1] and after drinking some tea, we boarded a small boat and headed out on the lake.

The hills were like a lady's dark eyebrows, and the flowers were like her cheeks. The gentle breeze was as intoxicating as wine, and the ripples were as soft as damask silk. I had barely lifted my head before I felt drunk and overwhelmed. At that moment I tried to describe it but found myself speechless. Probably Prince Tung-o felt exactly the same way when he first saw the goddess of the River Lo in his dream.[2] This was my first trip to West Lake. It was the fourteenth day in the second month of 1597, during the Wan-li reign.

Later in the day Tzu-kung[3] and I visited the Purity Temple, where we tried to locate the monk's lodge where Chung-tao used to stay. We came back passing by the Six Bridges, Yüeh's Tomb,[4] and the Stony Path Pond. We had only a brief look as we went along and didn't have the time to explore them.

The next morning I received a short note from T'ao Wang-ling.[5] On the nineteenth Wang-ling and his brother arrived, along with Wang Ching-hsü, a lay Buddhist. Hills and lakes, good friends—what great company at one and the same time!

Waiting for the Moon:
An Evening Trip to the Six Bridges

West Lake is at its best in springtime or in moonshine. In daytime it is at its best in the morning mist or in the evening glow.

This year it snowed heavily during the spring. The early plum [*Prunus mume*] trees, delayed by the snow, went into bloom along with the apricots and peaches. It was truly sensational. Wang-ling had told me several times that the early plum trees in the garden of Commander Fu of the Imperial Guard were formerly from Chang Kung-fu's Shining Jade Hall[1] and urged me to go there to have a look. But I was obsessed by the peach blossoms and couldn't bear to leave the view. On the lake, from the Broken Bridge[2] all the way to the Su Embankment, for some seven or eight miles, there stretched a mist in green and a haze of red. Wafted on the wind was the sound of music and singing. Perfumed perspiration fell like rain, and the sheen of silk and poplin outshone the grass along the embankment. It was the height of exquisite glamour.

Yet the people of Hangchow tour the lake from late morning until mid-afternoon only. In fact, the marvel of the lake and the color of the hills display themselves most fully at sunrise or right before sunset. At such moments the view is at the peak of its charm and voluptuousness. The moonlit scene is simply indescribable: flowers and willows, waters and hills —everything looks so different. Such pleasure is to be indulged in only by monks from the mountains and by travelers, and is certainly not to be divulged to the vulgar crowd!

A Trip to the Six Bridges after a Rain

It rained right after the Cold Food Day.[1] I said, "This rain is here to wash away the red [flowers] at West Lake. We should waste no time in bidding our farewell to the peach blossoms."

In the afternoon the rain stopped. I went to the Third Bridge with my friends, where the ground was covered by fallen petals more than an inch deep. To our delight, there were few tourists. Suddenly someone in white silk flitted by on horseback; the splendor of the whiteness was dazzling. All my friends who were wearing white clothes inside took off their outer garments.

Feeling a little sleepy, we lay down on the ground and had a drink. To amuse ourselves, we counted the flower petals falling onto our faces: those who received more would have to drink, and those who received less would have to sing. A small boat suddenly emerged from among the flowers. We called out and found it to be some Buddhist monks bringing tea from the temple. We all had a cup of tea and went home rocking our boat and singing loudly.

Mirror Lake

Mirror Lake used to be known as having a perimeter of some 260 miles.[1] Today there is no such a thing as a lake here anymore. Local residents said, "The lake used to be all over the farmland. But since those seaside flood-gates were built, the lake has turned into farmland."

Director Ho's Pond is less than a mile away from T'ao's Weir and is about two and a half miles in area. Wild grass stretched far and wide like a mist into the distance, and frogs croaked as if they were wailing; riding a boat on a moonlit night here made us feel quite forlorn.

Intoxicated, I said to Wang-ling, "You are not as unruly as Ho,[2] and you are not as much a drinker as Ho, but you have two eyes that approximate his." Wang-ling asked me why. I said, "Ho recognized the talent of the 'Banished Immortal.'[3] You've recognized that of Yüan Hung-tao. So you do have great vision, don't you?" Indignant at my crazy impudence, all those present fell silent.

A Trip to Brimming Well

It is cold in the Yen area.[1] Even after the Flowers Day Festival[2] the re-maining cold is still chilling. Often there is a freezing wind, and when it starts blowing, sand and gravel fly all around and one is confined to one's chamber, unable to go out. I sometimes try to ride out against the wind, but always turn back within a hundred steps.

On the twenty-second day, the weather was somewhat mild. I went out of the Eastern City Gate with a couple of friends and arrived at Brimming Well.[3] On both sides of the embankment there stood tall willow trees; the fertile soil there was slightly damp. Our vision extended far and wide, and I felt like a swan out of a cage. On that day a thin skin of ice had just started melting. Water sparkled, and ripples moved in layers and layers like fish scales. The fountain was so clear that we could see its very bottom, shining like the cold light from a mirror that had just been taken out of its case. Mountain peaks were washed by the snow in sunshine, looking fresh and bright, like a beautiful girl who has just washed her face and made up her hair. Willow twigs were about to bud, but not quite yet, with their tender tips trembling in the wind. In wheat fields the short mane of seedlings was about an inch high.

Although there were not too many tourists yet, we often ran into some who were drawing water from the fountain to make tea, some who were drinking and singing, or some women wearing red riding on donkeys. There was still a strong wind, but going on foot made us sweat all over. The birds who basked on the sands and the fish who sipped in the ripples were all at ease, and there emanated from their feathers and scales a cheerful freshness. Only then did I come to realize that outside in the suburbs and countryside, spring had already arrived, though it was hardly noticed by city dwellers.

Only because of the position I currently hold am I able to enjoy a good time among hills and woods, without having to worry about my official business being neglected on account of such excursions,[4] as this place happens to be close to my office. I shall start making my trips from now on. And how could I do so without putting it on record? It was in the second month of the year 1599.

A Trip to High Beam Bridge

High Beam Bridge is outside the Western City Gate.[1] It has the best view in the capital area. The embankment lies in the middle of water. Weeping willows extend for more than three miles. The river flows rapidly. The water is so clear that even the fins and scales of the fish at the bottom of the river can be seen. Buddhist temples dot the scene like pieces on a chessboard. Crimson towers and pearly pagodas beam among green trees. The Western Hills seem to be right within one's reach, enchanting tourists with their colors from morning till night. In the height of spring, gentlemen and ladies from the city gather there, and the crowd is thick as clouds. No government official would ever refrain from making a trip there unless he were extremely busy.

On the first day of the third month, I had an outing with Wang Chang-fu and the Buddhist monk Chi-tzu. A fresh green was sprouting at the tip of the willow branches. The hills shone from behind a thin mist. The river water rose up almost to the level of the embankment, and musicians were playing on their strings and pipes along both banks. Squatting on the root of an old tree, we drank some tea in place of wine, and, to accompany our drink, [in lieu of appetizers] we looked at the patterns of ripples and the shade of trees and watched, like a stage performance, the birds in the air, the fish in the water, and the people who walked back and forth.

Seeing the three of us sitting under the tree like fools, as if entranced in a Zen meditation, people who walked by along the embankment looked at one another and grinned. On our part, we were also wondering about those who were feasting and indulging themselves in a sound and fury that was totally out of tune with the charm and grace of mountains and rivers. What kind of pleasure could they really have? After a while I saw my class-mate[2] Huang Chai-chih, who came out to visit somebody, so I shouted to him, and he dismounted. We talked for a while. Then we took a walk to Sukhāvatī Temple to watch the early plum blossoms there before we went home.

A Biography of the Stupid but Efficient Ones

Master of Stone[1] observed, "No animal is more shrewd at running for refuge than the hare, yet it often falls into a hunter's hands. The cuttlefish spits ink to hide itself, and yet it often leads to its own destruction." What, then, is the advantage of being artful? The sparrow is not as good as the swallow in hiding itself, and the stork is not as good as the turtledove in providing for itself—it was already thus noted in old times.[2] I have there-fore written "A Biography of the Stupid but Efficient Ones."

There are four stupid servants in our family. They are Winter [Tung], East [Tung], Axe [Ch'i], and Hip [K'uei]. Winter is my servant. He has a retroussé nose, a flat face, blue eyes, a curly mustache, and a complexion of rusted iron. Once he went on a trip with me to Wu-ch'ang. On one occasion I sent him on a mission to someone in the neighborhood. On his way back he got lost. He walked back and forth several dozen times. He saw other ser-vants passing by but would not ask them for directions. At that time he was already over forty years old. I happened to go out and saw him looking all around in frustration, as if about to cry. I shouted to him, and he was over-joyed to see me. He likes to drink. One day, some wine was being brewed in the house. Winter begged for it and was given a cup. He was then sent away for something, so he just left it on the table. A maidservant stole the wine and drank it up. The wine brewer took pity on him and gave him another cup. While bending down toward the kitchen stove, Winter got caught in the flames, which flared across his face and almost burned his moustache and eyebrows. People in the house laughed, and he was given a bottle of wine. Delighted, Winter held the bottle in boiling water, planning on drinking it after it was warmed up. The boiling water splashed on him. He dropped the bottle and thus eventually did not get to drink a single drop of the wine. He left dumbfounded. Once someone told him to open a door, the hinges of which were somewhat tight. He pushed with all his might and fell down when the door opened. His head touched the ground while his feet flew up overhead. Everyone in the family roared with laughter. Earlier this year he went with me to my executive mansion in Peking. He had a good time with the gatekeepers there for half a year. Yet, on being asked the names of those people, he is at a total loss.

East also has an archaic appearance, but there is something funny about him. When he was young he served Tsung-tao. When Tsung-tao was about to marry his second wife, he told East to go buy some cakes in the city. Our house was more than thirty miles away from the city. The wedding date was close, so East was told to return in three days. Three days later, toward sunset he was not home yet. My father and Tsung-tao waited for him outside the gate. By evening they saw a person carrying something on a shoulder pole coming along the willow-lined embankment, and it turned out to be East. My father was delighted, so he led him back into the house in a hurry. The load was put down. They looked at it and found nothing but a jar of honey. They asked him where the cakes were. East replied, "I arrived in the city yesterday, and I happened to find the honey cheap, so I bought it. The cakes were expensive, really not worth buying." The next day had been fixed as the date to send over the betrothal gifts, but as a consequence it had to be postponed.

Both Axe and Hip are servants of the third brother [Chung-tao]. Once Axe went picking firewood. He knelt on the ground while tying the firewood into a bundle. He tied it so hard that the rope broke, and his fist hit his own breast. He was knocked out and fell to the ground, and stayed unconscious for quite a while. Hip looks like a buck. He is thirty years old, but he has not been "capped" yet.[3] His hair is tied up at the back of his head in a knotted braid that looks like a big rope. My younger brother gave him some money to buy a cap. Hip forgot that he kept a braid. After he came home, when he tied up his hair and put the cap on, his eyes and nose went into that cap. He sighed in astonishment for the rest of the day. One day he went to the next-door neighbor's and was chased by their dog. He put out his fists toward the dog as if he were about to fight another man and got his fingers bitten. It is just one example of his acts of folly.

However, while the cunning servants in our family have frequently been taken to task for wrongdoing, these four stupid ones have somehow managed to abide by the rules. One after another the cunning ones have been dismissed from the house. Without the means to provide for themselves, they could avoid hunger and starvation for no more than a year or two. The four stupid ones, on the other hand, having committed no wrong, are well fed and well clothed. Assured of their loyalty, the housekeeper has provided for each of them and would not see them leave the service. Aha! Shouldn't this suffice to demonstrate the efficacy of being stupid?

Essay: A Biography of Hsü Wen-ch'ang

One evening, while sitting upstairs at Grand Scribe T'ao's, I randomly pulled out something from his bookshelves and found it to be a portfolio of several volumes of poetry titled *A Collection of Scraps*. The paper was of poor quality, the calligraphy was slipshod, and soot had dimmed the printing, so the text was barely legible. I had to get closer to the lamp to read it. But after reading a few poems, I jumped up in surprise and cried out to Wang-ling, "Who's the author of this *Collection of Scraps*? Is he dead or alive?" Wang-ling replied, "This book was by Mr. Hsü Wen-ch'ang, a fellow townsman of mine." We both bounced up and down. We read and yelled, yelled and read in the lamplight, and all the servantboys who had fallen asleep were roused from their sleep. Alas! This untalented man here, my humble self, lived for thirty years before he got to know that there had been a Master Wen-ch'ang. Why did I come to know him so late? Therefore I now have put down all that I have heard from people of Yüeh in the following biography of Hsü Wen-ch'ang.

Hsü Wei, styled Wen-ch'ang, was already well known while a mere government student at Shan-yin. His Excellency Hsüeh Hui, while in charge of examinations in the Yüeh area, marveled at his genius and regarded him as a national star. Yet, as ill luck would have it, Hsü failed at every attempt in subsequent examinations. His Excellency Hu Tsung-hsien,[1] the vice censor-in-chief, heard about him and appointed him as a private secretary. Every time Wen-ch'ang went to meet His Excellency, wearing a black hood and a gown of hemp cloth, he would speak freely about state affairs, to the delight of His Excellency. At that time His Excellency was in command of several divisions of frontier troops and exercised great authority over the entire southeast. In front of His Excellency, those in armor and helmet would talk on their knees, bend over and walk with their faces down, and would not dare to lift their heads. But Wen-ch'ang, though only a government student on his staff, comported himself with dignity. People compared him to Liu T'an and Tu Fu.[2] Once, when the two white deer were captured, Wen-ch'ang was commissioned to write the memorial to the throne, and His Majesty the late emperor was delighted with it. His Excellency accordingly thought even more highly of him, and all His Excellency's memorials were composed by him. Wen-ch'ang took great pride in his knowledge of the art of war. He was fond of stratagems, and when he discussed military maneuvering he often would go right to the heart of the matter. He could not find anyone among contemporary men of letters who was his equal in talent, and yet he never had any luck.

Unsuccessful in his official career, Wen-ch'ang indulged himself in drinking and in enjoying the beauty of nature. He traveled in the regions of Ch'i, Lu, Yen, and Chao and explored the northern deserts. In his poetry he wrote about everything: undulating mountain ridges and hurling sea waves, whirling sands and floating clouds, howling wind and trees prostrate in it, the quiet mountain valley and the metropolis, human beings, fish and birds, and all kinds of events and things that surprised and amazed him. Deep down in his heart he always cherished unquenchable ambitions, but he also harbored the kind of sorrow felt by unfortunate heroic figures who have nowhere to turn for help. Accordingly, he took turns raging and laughing in his poetry. It is like riverwater roaring through the gorges, or sprouts bursting forth out of the soil. It is like a widow weeping at night, or a wayfarer sleepless in the cold. His poetry may be crude and unrefined in terms of structure at times, but, fresh and original, it has a lofty, princely manner that is not to be found in the works of those who assume an effeminate attitude waiting upon the delight of others. His prose writing, poised and well organized, shows great perception: its brilliance is unspoiled by imitation, and its eloquence remains unscathed by argumentation, placing its author in the same rank as Han and Tseng.[3] Wen-ch'ang never conformed to contemporary modes; rather, he rebuked all those who presided over the literary stage of his time and regarded them as inferiors. Hence his reputation did not spread beyond the Yüeh area. What a pity!

He liked to practice calligraphy. His brush strokes are bold and flowing like his poetry. Within its vigor and boldness there beam charm and elegance: it is like what Master Ou-yang[4] described as "a ravishing woman who is graceful even at old age." In leisure, his overflowing talent also drove him to try his hand at paintings of birds and flowers, which, unassuming and tasteful, are also superb.

Later, he killed his third wife when she aroused his suspicion. He was thrown into prison and sentenced to death, and was acquitted only after Grand Scribe Chang Yüan-pien's strenuous efforts to plead for him.[5] In old age he became even more resentful and tried even harder to feign madness. He sometimes shut his door on visitors of high station. He often took money and went to the tavern, where he would call lowbred attendants to join him for a drink. Once he hit and cracked open his own head with a hatchet; blood dripped all over his face. His broken skull creaked when his head was being rubbed. On another occasion he jabbed both his ears with a sharp awl, which penetrated about an inch and a half. But he survived.

Wang-ling said that his poetry and prose of the later period was even more remarkable. But, never having been printed, the collection has been kept in his family. A classmate of mine is now serving in the Yüeh area; I have asked him to obtain a handwritten copy for me, but it has not arrived yet. I have to make do with only *Hsü Wen-ch'ang's Works* and *A Collection of Scraps*. A social failure, Wen-ch'ang eventually passed away, carrying all his rage and regret into the grave.

Master of Stone observed, "Suffering from an endless series of bad luck, our master became insane. As a result of his insanity, he was thrown behind bars. Of all men of letters past and present who grieved and suffered, none was as miserable as our master. And yet His Excellency Hu was a hero of the age, and the late emperor was a sage sovereign. His Excellency, who treated the master in a way different from all the rest of his staff, must have understood him. When the memorial was presented, the sovereign was pleased, so His Majesty must have appreciated the master as well. What he missed was only rank and prestige. His poetry and prose, unequaled in his time, have swept away all the foul practice of our age. A hundred generations from now a fair evaluation will come around. So why should he be considered unappreciated and a failure? Mei K'o-sheng once wrote me a letter saying, 'Wen-ch'ang was an old friend of mine. His sickness was stranger than his personality; and his personality was stranger than his poetry.' I would rather say that nothing about Wen-ch'ang was not strange. And since nothing about him was not strange, he was out of luck wherever he went. How sad!"

Yüan Chung-tao (1570–1623)

Chung-tao, the youngest of the Yüan brothers, survived his two elder brothers and carried on the torch as an ardent champion of their literary ideas. Like his eldest brother, Tsung-tao, he was eclipsed in fame by Hung-tao. Chih-p'ing Chou, who called Chung-tao the "reformer of the Kung-an school," has pointed out that his views on literature deserve more critical attention.

Chung-tao was known as a child prodigy. At the early age of ten he was already the author of two lengthy rhapsodies, respectively on Yellow Mountain (Huang-shan) and on snow. But when he grew up, he was not enthusiastic about spending his time and energy on seeking an official career. Instead he traveled far and wide and, like Hung-tao, became a great admirer of the unorthodox thinker Li Chih, about whom he wrote a lively biography.

Urged by his brothers, Chung-tao did follow in their footsteps eventually and won first place in the provincial examination in 1603, when he was already thirty-three. Not until after the death of both his brothers did he finally receive the degree of Metropolitan Graduate in 1616, after which he served in a number of positions, including that of director in the Ministry of Personnel in Nanking.

The famous poet and critic Ch'ien Ch'ien-i, a good friend of Chung-tao's, gave us an account of how Chung-tao disliked the ideas of the so-called "Ching-ling school" led by Chung Hsing and T'an Yüan-ch'un, and thought about having an open debate with those "guys from Ch'u." He would never have imagined that he and his brothers would be thrown into the same category as Chung and T'an by some later literary historians. His prose, while not as dazzling as that of his brothers in originality, flows with ease and shows great emotion. The entries from his diaries presented here provide an early record of China's encounter with the West in a vivid portrait of the Jesuit missionary Matteo Ricci, as well as a realistic account of his brother Hung-tao's death.

Foreword to *The Sea of Misery*

Man's heart is like fire, and the predestined relationship of the world is like firewood. Experiencing sensual and pleasurable events is like the encounter of fire with dry firewood, to be further fueled by oil. If one manages to get rid of grease and oil, and splash cold water on the flame, then the fire will gradually burn out.

I have often seen how ambition for social success was set on fire by a person's leafing through documents of appointment, or how an aspiring mind was somewhat dampened by the sight of a funerary carriage. Our mind varies with circumstance, and my method of its cultivation may be of some use here. For this reason, people who retire from the world often live in the woods, where they may make use of impermanent waters to extinguish the blazing flame. This is the first secret to nurturing one's mind. Yüan Sung, who was fond of singing a funerary dirge, also had that in mind.[1] Being a smart person, he was only using it to cool his own youthful ambitions. Yet it was regarded as an idiosyncrasy, which really missed the point.

In the past I was in pursuit of many worldly things and constantly cherished all kinds of wild aspirations. Later I gathered in this collection poems of past and present that lament for the living and mourn for the dead, and have titled it *The Sea of Misery*. To chant these pieces aloud at times of heat and flame may remind us of the scarcity of the rest of our days and the impermanence of prosperity, so the crackling fire might be transformed into a cold, refreshing cloud. Whenever I suffer from such fever, I use it as a prescription, and it has always worked. I would like to make it known far and wide in the world to help people in their fever and misery. It is really a matter of transcendence,[2] so I would like to have it preserved. On an autumn day in 1585, Yüan Chung-tao, the Chime-maker,[3] has just written the above in a boat.

Shady Terrace

Our residence in the suburbs of Ch'ang-an[1] has a garden on its left where old pine trees abound. Behind the gate there flows a clear stream, and a grove of slender bamboos grows along its banks. Across the bridge there is a scholar-tree [*Sophora japonica*] that reaches to the sky, even the twigs of which would be considered tall trees in themselves in other mountains. There are also trees of other kinds, such as peach, plum [*Prunus salicina*], date, and chestnut, all dense and luxuriant.

There are three rows of rooms for studying, where my two elder brothers and I prepared for our examinations together. They made their degree of Metropolitan Graduate one after the other and moved into the city with their families; I alone have lived here since. In summertime, having nothing else to do, I had a terrace built by the stream under the scholar-tree; the terrace was covered in its green shade and sheltered from the sunshine all the time, so I named it Shady Terrace.

I often invite friends to come over and have some fun here. There are no spectacular peaks or deep valleys in view, but over the hills and ranges, far and near, thick pines and green bamboos grow lush. Whenever a wind arises from afar, it comes over winding through the thousands of pine trees until its raging force has been spent and it comes to a stop here. Then it joins in the breeze that comes over from the lotus flowers in the pond, so there is always a faint coolness and fragrance. At sunset one has to wear double-layered clothes to sit outside there. Looking down, I can see fish frolicking; raising my head, I can listen to birds chirping. Elated, I always shout to my friends, "Isn't this the place for a recluse?"

Selections from *Wood Shavings of Daily Life*

1

Late at night it snowed a little more heavily. I had planned to make a boat trip to Sha-shih, but gave up because of the rain and snow. Yet it was somewhat nice to hear the snow pellets tinkling among thousands of bamboos and to read a few chapters by the dim light from the window and the red glow of fire. I often regret that I've not been able to carry out my travel plans, but one should really go on with the flow of the stream, and stop when an islet lies ahead—just take it easy. As Huang T'ing-chien said, "Wherever I go, I'm able to have a nice dream."

2

Hosted a banquet for all the guests who came to celebrate the launching of the new boat. Strings, woodwinds, and percussion sounded in tune. We had the boat rowed upriver against the current. Spectators stood like walls. The reflection from the surface of water was a shining sheet of light. The sound of singing, talking, and laughing sank into the waves. By dusk, dark clouds rose in all directions. We had the boat rowed back to where it had been. There was a windstorm. Guests and messengers scattered like meteors. Throughout that night, the river roared as in an earthquake.

3

In the gazette I read the obituary of Li Ma-tou [Matteo Ricci], an Attendant from the West.[1] Ma-tou had come from his native country by sea; it took him four or five years to arrive. At first he stayed in Fukien, and then in Wu and Yüeh. By and by he learned to speak and read Chinese. Later he went to the capital and presented the portrait of the Master of Heaven [God] and the chime clock that he had brought with him. The imperial court offered him board and lodging. In his country, people serve Heaven and know nothing about Buddha. They do good deeds and treasure friendship. Many people remain virginal all their life. Ma-tou was quite eloquent and also good at writing. He had a low income, but he often gave money to others. He purchased a house, employed servants, and lived well. People suspected that he, like Wang Yang,[2] knew some secret alchemy. Ma-tou was indeed conversant with many special skills, but regretfully they'll remain unknown. He has said that the celestial body is like an egg, the sky being its white and the earth its yolk, and that there are worlds above and beneath us and in all four directions. He has also remarked that the people of the world above and the people of the world below have their feet against each other's, because the latter are like flies or insects moving upside down on roof beams. These sayings are very strange, but they accord with the *Miscellaneous Flowers Sūtra:* "Facing upward there is a world, facing down there is a world, and looking sideways there is a world." Ma-tou made friends with officeholders. I saw him several times at Hung-tao's executive mansion. He lived to only sixty. I was told that he died a virgin.

4

On the night of the sixth[1] the old maidservant in Hung-tao's room suddenly cried out to me and asked me to go in, saying, "He urinated three or four times at night—each time passing blood—and he almost fainted. If the urine stops, then maybe he could talk." I wept in private. She comforted me. We hurried to call in Li, the doctor, who felt his pulse and said, "The pulse is slowing down." I stamped my feet and threw myself on the ground. The doctor said, "Don't panic! Let's try ginseng soup." After taking the ginseng he started gasping and said that he was three-tenths alive but seven-tenths dead. After a while he got up to urinate again and murmured to himself, "I'll take a nap." He didn't say anything else, and just passed away sitting there. When I called out to him, he could no longer respond! Alas! Alas! So just overnight, I lost my dear brother! The sky and earth fell apart. I would have been happy to die together with him. I didn't want to live in the world anymore. I fell on the ground in a faint and remained unconscious for a long time. Then I managed to get up to take care of preparation for the burial. There were only fifty taels of silver in his money bag. I had to beg for a loan and pawn something to purchase the coffin. I had never realized that a director of the Ministry of Personnel could be in such straitened circumstances! In grief I went up to Kung-an to console our old father.

5

I took a walk by the river and watched the thousands of acres of white sand on the northern bank that looked like snow. That night I was very sad. Since Hung-tao's death all those who claimed to be bosom friends among his classmates have said something against him in contempt or indignation. In the middle of the night I read aloud the observation of "Dragon Pool" Li [Li Chih]: "Common men are free from falsity, so they are unable to conceal their true heart. Men who talk about the Tao have lost their innocence, so they are determined to purge those who stand out among them." This saying is indeed as invaluable as Yü's Tripod or the Mirror of Ch'in![1]

Chung Hsing (1574–1624)

A native of Ching-ling County in Hu-kuang, Chung Hsing is known in literary history, along with his younger fellow townsman and bosom friend T'an Yüan-ch'un, as founder of the Ching-ling school, one of the contending literary groups in early seventeenth-century China.

The son of a county school supervisor, Chung Hsing passed the prefectural examination in 1603 after many unsuccessful attempts and eventually won the degree of Metropolitan Graduate in 1610, as a classmate of Ch'ien Ch'ien-i. He was then appointed a Messenger (Hsing-jen), a member of a central government agency whose principal function was to deliver formal, nonroutine documents to important dignitaries, such as enfeoffed princes or foreign tributary chiefs. In this position Chung traveled to Shantung, Szechwan, and even Kweichow Province on the southwestern frontier.

Between his subsequent various appointments, mostly insignificant, Chung spent much time behind closed doors in Nanking, avidly reading Confucian classics and historical works and trying his best to stay away from the partisan struggles of various political factions during the Wan-li reign. At his last appointment, as assistant superintendent of education at Fukien, he was impeached and dismissed from office.

Possibly because of family tragedies (the deaths of his younger brother and his sixteen-year-old only son) as well as his frustration with the politics of his time, Chung turned to serious reading of Buddhist sūtras in his late forties. He adopted a vegetarian diet and wrote a book of explication on the Surangama Sūtra. *On his deathbed he was formally initiated into full monkhood.*

In his lifetime Chung established a reputation as a poet, historian, and landscape painter, but his influence was felt less in these achievements than in his literary criticism, which advocated the importance of hard thinking in the composition process, in search of the mentality or "true spirit" of ancient poets. This theory is exemplified in the two popular anthologies of classical and T'ang poetry that Chung compiled in collaboration with T'an Yüan-ch'un. The modern Chinese scholar Ch'ien Chung-shu has argued that in the field of poetry and poetics the influence of the Ching-ling school was in fact greater and more lasting than that of the Kung-an school. Chung admired the Yüan brothers and the theory of the Kung-an school, especially the concept of "natural sensibility," but accused their followers of crudity and superficiality. Ironically, Chung and T'an may have tried a little too hard in rectifying the weakness of the Kung-an school. They were charged with affectation and obscurity by later critics, to a large extent because of their laborious experimentation with diction and syntax, as exemplified in the long sentence at the opening of "Flower-Washing Brook," which approaches the spirit of Ernest Hemingway's page-long, unpunctuated sentences. Chung's prose generally assumes a serious tone, but occasionally, as in "Inscription on My Portrait," it also reveals his humor and wit.

Flower-Washing Brook

Outside the southern gate of Ch'eng-tu, the Bridge of Ten Thousand Li[1] is on the left. There, turning westward, slender, lengthy, in graceful twists and turns; looking like a chain of linked rings, like a jade circle, like a girdle, like a roundel, like a hook; shining in its dark, deep green color like a mirror, like gemstone, like a dark green melon; and winding its way around and beneath the city wall, is the Flower-Washing Brook, which all of the tributaries converge into. Only after one comes to the Thatched Lodge, however, is the stream there known specifically as the Flower-Washing Brook, because that is where Tu Fu's Flower-Washing Cottage is located.[2]

About a mile ahead there stands the Black Sheep Palace.[3] The brook is sometimes close by and sometimes in the distance. It is verdant with bamboo and cypress along the shore. The brook disappears into the dark depth across the bank. As one looks straight ahead, the ground seems to be covered by shepherd's purse [*Capsella bursa-pastoris*]. The water is clear, the plants lush: the view is refreshing and stimulating both to the spirit and to the flesh. West of the palace the tributaries converge, and there are three bridges with only less than three hundred yards of distance in between. I was told by the sedan-chair carrier that it leads all the way to Kuan-hsien. Perhaps this refers to the line "The river comes all the way from Kuan-k'ou."[4] Some houses stand on the left of the brook, so the brook is sometimes invisible, but now and then it emerges again. It is like that at several places. Firewood is tied up in bundles and bamboo is woven into fences; everything is neatly arranged.

Across the last bridge a gazebo stands on the left of the road, with an inscription that reads "Riverside Road." After that is the Commandant's Shrine.[5] In front of the shrine a plank bridge, with a balustrade with posts standing in the water, spans the brook. What comes into view next is a horizontal board with the inscription "Flower-Washing Brook." Across the bridge an islet lies crisscross in the water; surrounded by the brook, it is accessible only by the bridge. A gazebo stands on the islet, with the inscription "Waters from Hundred Flowers Pool." Back from this gazebo, across the bridge and past Fan-an Temple, there stands at last Vice-Director Tu's Shrine.[6] The portrait is pretty tasteful, but it could be mere imagination—verisimilitude is irrelevant, anyway. There is a portrait on a stone monument, with a biography attached to it. It was made when administrative aide Ho Jen-chung served as acting prefect of Hua-yang. The inscription is hardly legible.

Master Chung observed that of the two residences of Tu the Senior,[7] Flower-Washing is secluded and Eastern Garrison difficult of access, varying in style. If His Excellency Yen [Wu] were not deceased, Flower-Washing Lodge would have been an ideal place for retirement. How important it is to have a friend in need! Yet it must have been Heaven's desire to send this old man here to add some luster to such a spectacular place like K'uei-meng![8] Even while running about in frustration and misery, he could still choose to live in places with a great view and was capable of keeping equilibrium in his heart to cope with the vicissitudes of the world. It was like when Confucius was in exile and served in disguise as the housekeeper of Ssu-ch'eng Chen-tzu.[9] It was the seventeenth day of the tenth month of 1611, during the Wan-li reign. When I went beyond the city wall it was about to rain, but it cleared up after a while. Most of those who came here on imperial errands and toured the place were invited by local officials to join the drinking party. It was crowded with all of the officials and their carriages. People made deep bows to one another in greeting, making much noise; toward dusk they hurried back. I happened to go there alone early in the morning.

The above note was written by Chung Hsing, a native of Ch'u.[10]

To Ch'en Chi-ju

It was indeed a marvelous predestined event for the two of us to meet each other, though I somehow regret that it didn't occur earlier. Yet, if we had met ten years ago, I'm afraid that, not having as much insight and perception as we do today, we would not have been able to inspire and stimulate each other as now. It is not an easy thing for friends to meet. Frankly, I also believe that we should not be afraid of missing each other, but rather of seeing each other without acquiring something that is mutually beneficial. Since much good has come from our meeting, why should I still regret that it didn't occur earlier?

A Colophon to My Poetry Collection

Li Ch'ang-shu once told me, "Men like you are great, but you just read too much, and you are too good at writing poetry and prose. If you could give up reading and writing, then you'd become full-fledged notables."[1] I replied in disappointment, "Aha! How nice! None except you could have said something like that; and none except I could have understood what you just said. What a pity those who would resent it are unable to understand it. If they could understand it, they would be more eager to kill you than to kill me. However, though I'm capable of admiring what you said, I'll never be capable of practicing it. You should take back what you said and practice it by yourself. Maybe someday in the future I'll practice what you said."

A few days later I showed the above to [T'an] Yüan-ch'un. Yüan-ch'un wrote back, "What Ch'ang-shu said was nice, what you said about Ch'ang-shu was even nicer, and what I now say about you two is just as nice!"

Both of us are addicted to reading and poetry writing, and yet we could admire someone's suggestion about giving up reading and writing. Those who could make such a suggestion, then, certainly would not dismiss reading and writing altogether! Yüan Hung-tao once remarked, "People like us cannot live a day without poetry and prose." I agree. There was a man who inquired about the secret of longevity. The answer was, "Just hold back your desires." The man shook his head and said, "If so, then what's the good of living a thousand years?" What pleasure in life is there for people like us if we have to refrain from writing poetry and prose? Although I admire but cannot carry out what Ch'ang-shu suggested, I'm sure Ch'ang-shu does not consider me wrong. But even if he really does, I'll just have to let him do as he pleases.

A Colophon to *A Drinker's Manual* (Four Passages)

First, spirit. In the tumult of clinking huge drinking horns, allowing the spirit to lapse into disorder will surely reduce the pleasure. On the other hand, behaving in a reserved and solemn manner departs even further from the true realm [of drinking]. A good drinker behaves just as usual, because his spirit is always at ease. Ts'ao Ts'ao,[1] on the eve of a battle, appeared as if he had no desire for a fight. During the battle of Fei-shui, Hsieh An spent his time at his villa playing chess for a wager.[2] How could anyone do without such a spirit in drinking?

Second, vital force. Predators command by their vital force; therefore, small predators are capable of preying upon larger animals. In the battle-field of drinking, if one does not have the kind of vital force that would enable one to dash into enemy troops with no fear, then one's throat is surely going to suffer in swallowing a hundred goblets or an entire *tan*[3] of wine. I once held a huge drinking horn and challenged the guests around the table. All the tipplers there were intimidated, but those who took pride in their capacity for liquor were also excited and ready to try their best. In the field of drinking, holding the vital force may caution the headstrong and embolden the timid.

Third, zest. It is a misery indeed to succumb to the enfeebling addiction of drink; yet how can anyone know the pleasure of drinking if he sinks into a lethargy or yells to himself in a stupor? Only those who are superb in the art of sobriety know how to stay away from the torture of drinking and to indulge in its pleasure. Those who are able to remain on the brink of intox-ication are especially rare in attaining exquisite pleasure. Li Po said, "If you understand the zest of drinking / Don't share it with the sober ones."[4] Here he is referring only to those who are sober by abstinence. It is an entirely different story for those who are superb in the art of sobriety.

Fourth, moderation. "In drinking, Master does not keep count, but he always stays within limits."⁵ To do as you please, to go easy by the golden mean, isn't that the way of the sage? "Give me a *tou*, and I'll get intoxicated; give me a *tan*, and I'll get intoxicated, too."⁶ This turns out to be in accordance with Confucius's family instruction. Because it follows the way of nature, it is the key to keeping oneself within bounds.

Inscription after Yüan Hung-tao's Calligraphy

We all try to model after the ancients in writing poetry and prose, and the spirit of the ancients is sustained in poetry and prose passed down in handwritten or printed copies. Yet, when we try to model after the ancients in practicing calligraphy, their spirit is nowhere to be found except in original handwriting or in old rubbings from stone tablets, and how many originals or old rubbings are extant today? Hence I suspect that those of superior taste frequently practice calligraphy by following their own gusto rather than by modeling after the ancients, simply because there are no ancients around to model after. Since there are no ancients around to model after, it is better for those of superior taste to follow their own gusto rather than to pretend to model after the ancients.

I venture to verify my argument with Yüan Hung-tao's calligraphy. There are a variety of skills and techniques in the world. For those related to the use of implements, there is a difference between ingeniousness and clumsiness, and for those related to the use of brush and ink, there is a difference between elegance and vulgarity. The matter of ingeniousness or clumsiness is something that one can learn to improve, but the matter of elegance or vulgarity is not. Hung-tao passed away little more than a decade ago. His calligraphy is by no means accomplished. But now, as I unroll the scroll and gaze at it, it looks like an ancient relic thousands of years old that has suddenly emerged in our world. Why is it so? Please deliberate upon it with calligraphers.

Inscription on My Portrait

When the god of the sea was about to meet the emperor of Ch'in, he asked for a pledge, saying, "I am ugly. Do not have anyone portray me." The pledge was given. Someone who waited upon the emperor tried to draw, with his toes, a sketch of the Sea God. The Sea God was furious. Surging tidal waves chopped the bank, and he said, "The emperor has betrayed me!"

This is an example of how everyone, by nature, wants to look nice and to keep the unsightly to oneself. I am haggard, and not handsome at all. Those who met me were often disappointed. Hu Chün-p'ing from Chiangling drew my portrait and is about to take it away with him. P'ei Tu,[1] the duke of Chin, once said, "Seeing that I am wrecked with age, he purposely makes fun of me." Now I beg to offer myself, delicately built like a reed or a catkin willow, to win a chuckle from Chün-p'ing and his brothers.

Li Liu-fang (1575–1629)

Li Liu-fang received the degree of Provincial Graduate in 1606, in the same year as Ch'ien Ch'ien-i. Four years later Ch'ien won third place in the metropolitan examination (with Chung Hsing among his classmates), but Li was passed over. In 1622 Li was to make another attempt, but, due to adverse travel conditions had reached only the suburbs of Peking when the examination started inside the city.

The corrupt eunuch Wei Chung-hsien (1568–1627) had quickly risen to power with the enthronement of Emperor Hsi-tsung (r. 1621–27). At the peak of his authority Wei incited his supporters to have shrines honoring himself built throughout the empire. Li refused to participate in the worship, saying, "To do the service is a matter of an instant; not to do it is a matter of a thousand ages." He gave up his ambition for an official career, went back south, and built a villa—the Sandalwood Garden at Nan-hsiang, in the southeastern part of his native county, Chia-ting, Southern Metropolitan Region—for his old mother and himself. Together with his son Hang-chih, a talented painter, Li personally saw to the planting and placement of all the trees and rocks in the garden.

In this beautiful garden Li Liu-fang entertained his friends, including his classmate Ch'ien Ch'ien-i, who had asked for leave on the excuse of ill health and returned to live in nearby Ch'ang-shu County. Here Li devoted himself to calligraphy, painting, poetry, and the study of Taoism. He also made frequent trips for sightseeing and painting in the Chiang-nan area, especially to Soochow and Hangchow.

Today Li is remembered first of all as an accomplished landscape painter, known as one of the Nine Painter Friends, a group headed by Tung Ch'i-ch'ang, the great master of the age, and immortalized in a poem by the famous poet Wu Wei-yeh (1609–72). The bold brushwork and rich ink tones of Li's paintings display grace and spontaneity as well as the influence of various masters of the Yüan dynasty, especially Huang Kung-wang (1269–1354) and Wu Chen (1280–1354).

Though leading a recluse's life, Li still cared about affairs of state and had a *tragic sense of the doom of the Ming imperial reign. In 1629, when he heard that Ch'ien Ch'ien-i, who after the death of Wei Chung-hsien had returned to the capital and become a high-ranking courtier, was dismissed, Li sighed and said that the situation for the empire was now hopeless. Soon he fell sick, started coughing up blood, and died shortly.*

Su Shih, the great Sung writer, made a famous saying about the achievements of Wang Wei (701–61), the great T'ang poet and painter: "In his poetry, one feels that there is painting. In his painting, one sees that there is poetry." One may say the same thing about Li Liu-fang's landscape paintings and his hsiao-p'in *pieces.*

A Short Note about My Trips to Tiger Hill

Tiger Hill is most frequented by tourists on the night of the Mid-Autumn Festival.[1] Gentlemen and ladies of the entire city go out there. The sound of music and talk, filling up the vales and bubbling in the woods, continues throughout the night. The entire place is turned into a tavern, and I am often disgusted by such rowdiness.

I arrived at the prefecture on the tenth, and went to Tiger Hill that very night. The moonshine was grand, and there were few tourists. The gazebos in the breeze and the waterside pavilions in the moonlight, adorned by a group or two that included some rouge-cheeked singing girls, were surely not repulsive at all.

Still it was not as agreeable to me as when I went there alone, when the hill was deserted and quiet. One autumn evening I sat by the Moon-fishing Jetty with Jo-sheng. It was very dark, and no one walked by. From time to time we heard the sound of bells in the wind, and saw the light on and off from the Buddhist temple above the trees. On another occasion during the past spring, I called upon Chung-ho here together with my nephew Wu-chi. At midnight the moon rose and no one else was around. Together we squatted on the stone terrace. We neither drank nor talked. Contemplating the scene with a detached mind, we felt as if we had imperceptibly become a part of the exquisitely tranquil landscape.

I think there have been only two occasions in my life when I visited Tiger Hill and saw its natural beauty. To quote the lines of my friend Hsü Sheng-yüan,

Only the depth of winter reveals things at their best;[2]
And they are singularly suited to visits at midnight.

He knew the secret, indeed!

A Short Note about My Trips to Boulder Lake

In the past I have visited Boulder Lake[1] three times, and had a great time on all three trips.

In 1575 Fang-ju and I put on clogs and went there in the rain. We climbed to the gazebo on the summit of the hill, where we drank some wine, sang wildly, and shouted at the top of our voices. All those who saw us stared.

Last year Meng-yang,[2] Jo-sheng, Kung-yü, and I went there looking for early plum [*Prunus mume*] in bloom. We toured all the buildings at Chih-p'ing Temple, climbed up the Sacrificial Terrace, and went to Shang-fang Temple at the summit. There was a refreshing breeze, the sun was bright, and we had a very nice time.

On the ninth, we went there again for "height-ascending,"[3] but due to a rain didn't climb up the hill. We went on the lake in our boat and watched all the masts, sails, and oars coming and going in the rain. We had a drink while enjoying the view, and it was very pleasant.

On this trip it was a bright and clear autumn day. My younger brother Po-mei and others were all in a good mood. We went up to Shang-fang via Vetch Village, and then we found a way to come down via the Sacrificial Terrace and the Tea Mill. Wildflowers growing by the roadside often sent out a soft, sweet scent; some of our boys picked up armfuls of them. At sunset we let our boat stay in the middle of the lake and waited for the moon to rise. We were about to start drinking when Meng-yang and Lu-sheng arrived one after the other. We sat on the boat in the dew, drank a lot, and didn't return until midnight. I had not had such a nice time for a decade!

Inscriptions on *An Album of Recumbent Travels in Chiang-nan* (Four Passages)

Horizontal Pond

Three miles outside the Hsü Gate[1] there is a village by the name of Horizontal Pond. It is a lovely place indeed, with low and smooth hills around, the pond affording an unobstructed view, and bridges and streams lying between villages. Every time I passed by, I felt as if the city were receding farther and farther away and that the lake and hills there were very friendly. My heart felt lifted up, as if the fresh wind and bright sunshine were there for my sake, though my fellow travelers were unable to feel the same kind of ecstasy.

Above Horizontal Pond is Horizontal Hill. P'an Fang-ju and I were once stopped there en route by a windstorm. We found our way to the foot of the hill. There were elegant pines and bamboos, and the small peach trees were just in bloom. It looked almost like a wonderland. We helped each other climb to the top of the hill. The wind was extremely strong. We felt as if we would be blown off our feet and fall down. That was twenty years ago.

In 1617, three days after the Mid-Autumn Fesitval, I painted this picture at Meng-yang's residence by the Ch'ang Gate. In the ninth month I made another trip to Wu-lin in the company of Meng-yang.[2] It rained at night. I wrote this inscription while our boat was moored at Chu's Cape.

Boulder Lake

Boulder Lake is below Mount Leng-ch'ieh. The Buddhist temple at the summit is named Shang-fang. Along the winding path to the east, where the hills become lower but more undulating, stand the Sacrificial Terrace and the Tea Mill. The temple beneath the Sacrificial Terrace is named Chih-p'ing. The bridge that spans the lake is called the Spring Walk. The bridge across the streams, which leads to the winery, is called Yüeh-lai. The lake is about three miles away from the city. Easily accessible to tourists, it is most popular for "height-ascending" parties; gentlemen and ladies from the city gather there.

On the Double Ninth in 1608, Meng-jan and I made a trip there. It happened to be windy and rainy; there were few tourists. The hills and the lake looked newly washed. We put on clogs and went to Chih-p'ing Temple, and stayed there until dusk. I wrote a poem on the occasion:

On the Double Ninth, full of thoughts of home,
A traveler has come here to watch the hills in rain.
Unable to reach the summit of the mountain,
We just moor our boat in the western bay.
Above the Tea Mill a white mist soars up in the wind;
At Vetch Village the foliage takes on a splendid hue.
Who'd say this is not a cap-dropping party[1]
At which we shall not return before we get drunk?

Beneath the mountain is Purple Vetch Village. Meng-jan used to live there, but he is gone forever now. Alas!

Tiger Hill

Tiger Hill fits in nicely with the moon, with snow, with rain, with mist, with dawn in spring, with summer, with the refreshing cool of autumn when the leaves are falling, and with the setting sun. It is nice for all such moments, but it is never nice when there is a crowd of tourists. Its misfortune comes from being situated close to the city. Tourists frequent the place, like those attracted by the smell of mutton or "addicted to the stench of body odor,"[1] not because they really understand the pleasure of sight-seeing.

In the eighth month of this year, Meng-yang passed by Soochow. I took a boat ride to meet him. On the night of the Mid-Autumn Festival, the moon did not come out. On the sixteenth it cleared up by night, so we made a trip to Tiger Hill together, but couldn't get close to it because of the crowd and the filth—we left holding our noses. Today, when I put down this inscription for Meng-yang, the hills and the woods have emerged in their natural look.

On the sixth day of the ninth month in 1617, I wrote this note en route to Clear Brook.

Divinity Cliff

On my trips to Western Hill, I passed by the foot of Divinity Cliff Hill (Ling-yen-shan) several times. On an autumn day in 1608 I finally got to ascend the hill with Ch'i-tung and his two sons, Liang-chan and Jung-chan. On all the previous occasions, I had only watched from aboard my boat the pretty view of its woods and rocks in the distance.

Divinity Cliff is the site of the Belle's Lodge.[1] The Footfall Corridor, the Flower-Picking Trail, and the Zither Terrace are all located there. On one of the rocks there is a depression that looks like a footprint. It is said to be the track left by Hsi Shih's shoe, which is hard to believe. When I was young, I once dreamt that my friends and I went to the Buddhist shelters there to compose poems. On waking up I still remembered one line: "Wind among the pines, moon on water: both have the power of speech." In 1611, on our way to watch early plum in bloom at Western Moraine, my younger brother and I passed by Divinity Cliff. I wrote a poem with a reference to that dream:

> The rain keeps falling beneath Divinity Cliff;
> Flower Trail and Zither Terrace are enveloped in cloud.
> I remember the autumn hills and the yellow leaves on the road;
> Wind among the pines, moon on water: message of Zen in a
>   dream.

On the seventh day of the ninth month in 1617, I wrote this inscription in a boat on Western Pond.

Inscription on *A Picture of Solitary Hill on a Moonlit Night*

Once, after getting drunk in the company of Monk Yin-ch'ih and several brothers, we took a little boat on our way back from the West Fall.[1] The moon had just risen, and the branches of the weeping willows on the new embankment were all reflected on the lake, vibrating in that open sheet of light. It was like a scene in a mirror or in a picture.

I have always cherished that scene in my memory. In 1612, while staying in the villa, one day I was suddenly tempted to put it in a painting for Meng-yang. Now it is really in a picture.

Wang Ssu-jen (1575–1646)

A native of beautiful Shan-yin County in Chekiang, Wang Ssu-jen was the son of an herb doctor with a government appointment. Known as a child prodigy, Wang received the degree of Provincial Graduate in 1594. Only a year later, at the age of twenty, he won the degree of Metropolitan Graduate and made instantaneous literary fame.

A humorist by nature in the tradition of the legendary Ch'un-yü K'un, Yen Ying, and Tung-fang So, Wang Ssu-jen offended a great number of nobles by his offhand witty remarks on politics and politicians. This probably had a negative impact on his official career, which went through many ups and downs and was generally insignificant. During fifty years of government service, Wang was out of office more than half of the time.

After Peking fell to the rebels and the Ming empire came to a tragic end with Emperor Ssu-tsung's suicide, Wang was summoned from his retirement and appointed minister of rites in the short-lived regency regime of the prince of Lu at Shao-hsing, Chekiang. When the Manchu troops arrived in Shan-yin, where Wang was living in retirement, behind closed doors he kept writing in big characters "No Surrender," refused to cut his hair in the new style as demanded by the Manchu regime, and died from fasting.

A versatile man, Wang was also known as a poet, painter, and calligrapher. As an essayist he explored the possibilities of prose through writing a chronological autobiography (the first of its kind in Chinese literature), a humorous book of chess (wei-ch'i; Japanese go) regulations, and a book about his travels in the Chekiang mountains entitled Wanderlust *(Yu-huan), which has become a classic in its own right. His travel writings were widely acclaimed even in his lifetime. Both Ch'en Chi-ju and the great playwright T'ang Hsien-tsu (1550–1616) were his admirers; both wrote laudatory forewords for his collections of prose. Chang Tai wrote a vivid biographical sketch of him. His travel notes, always refreshing and highly expressive, are among the very best of the genre.*

A Trip to Brimming Well

The capital is a thirsty place. Where there is water, there is fun. A little more than a mile and a half outside the An-ting Gate is the Brimming Well. In early spring, gentlemen and ladies gather there like clouds.

I went there to have a look with Chang Tu, a friend from Wu. The well, about five and a half feet in diameter, is encased in a gazebo. The water surface is higher in the middle than on the four sides, hence the name. The way it brims is that the fountain surges and gurgles like a string of beads, like crabs' eyes agape, or the foamy bubbles of fish. The lush vines and grass around it sustain its moisture.

Visitors included all kinds of people, from powerful eunuchs and nobles on down. Some were wearing caps, and some headcloths. Some were carrying loads with a pole, and some on their back. Some were sitting on the grass. Some were holding on to one another by neck or shoulder, scattering their shoes around them. A clamor of voices filled the air. Some were hawking drink and food with hollers of "Great hot cakes!" "Great wine!" "Great big dumplings!" "Great fruit!" The rich and the poor each had their own supplies. The powerful ones sat closer to the well and the insignificant stayed farther away. Hired thugs, swollen with arrogance, blustered people away from their masters. Fathers and sons and husbands and wives were drinking toasts to each other. Women with towering coiffures and sprawling hair-buns were looking around for their missing shoes and earrings. There were also those who raged and cursed after getting drunk, got into trouble, and then apologized humbly or begged for mercy. It is known that once a woman gave birth to a child while sitting there, surrounded by old women who took off their short jackets and held them up as curtains. Under the glances of thousands of people, these women held one another's hands and smiled.

What I witnessed included one who swooned and was carried away, her limp body lying across the back of a donkey; a carrier who missed the stirrup of his horse, fell flat on his back, and made a fool of himself before the public; some who swaggered and bullied others, robbing the articles or clothes of one and harassing the wife or daughter of another; and some who stood up to defend the victims, went into a bloody fight, and got themselves injured or [maybe] even killed. The entire place turned into a pandemonium. My friend Chang and I had a drink in the shade of a reed umbrella and didn't leave until we had seen enough of this circus show.

A Trip to Wisdom Hill and Tin Hill

To a native of Yüeh on his way home from the north, seeing Tin Hill in the distance is like seeing his own family. To look at the blue stroke that crosses half the sky is like getting a drink after having been thirsty for a long time. As for a drink that comes from under the ground, there is nothing better than that from the spring at Wisdom Hill. All residents in that area are from the Chiang family.[1]

In the market the wine made with water from the spring was fantastic. A woman with a relaxed and detached look ran a business there; I enjoyed visiting her place to buy clay statuettes, folded-paper chickens, carved-wood tigers, masks from Lan-ling, as well as some toy swords and halberds to give to my kids. As for her wine, she provided clean porcelain cups and allowed me a taste first before the bargain. I asked for the clear, refreshing kind, and she said that she would choose and present to me a pastry to go with the wine. How could a man drink wine along with that sweet stuff? What a sweetheart—just worth dying for! Shen Ch'iu-ho remarked, "If Wen-chün indeed were presiding over the tavern, then where should Hsiang-ju be positioned?"[2] We went into the temple and paid homage to Buddha. After that we scooped some water from the fountain and drank it.

Together we went to the summit of Wisdom Hill. There we looked at the vast Lake T'ai-hu. The county loomed in the distance, beyond wild ducks and wild geese flying across multicolored clouds. Below the hill there was a full-scale marketplace with fresh fish and meat that was nowhere to be found in Yangchow and Nanking. After dining we went to have a look at the Fool's Valley Garden, which was already a barren waste. The spring there was still gurgling, but it was not like Ch'in's Garden, which still had clean, sprawling rocks and lush, graceful old trees.

We went westward up Tin Hill. There we looked down at the city. Rows and rows of houses lined together like fish scales. Green rivers circled around and through them, as on a piece of embroidery. It was indeed a blessed land in the Wu area. Right after the construction of the Buddhist temples Sun, one of the top three Metropolitan Graduates, emerged; and at their reconstruction Hua, the Principal Candidate, appeared.[3] So it seems that the terrestrial veins indeed exist![4]

When we returned to our boat, visitors kept coming. People sang and played all kinds of music. It was like hearing divine tunes while floating in multicolored clouds. Suddenly it was as if Yeh Fa-shan were holding the hands of the Third Brother and Yü-huan, and guiding them to walk across the Bridge of the Crescent Moon for a sightseeing tour of the lanterns of Kuang-ling.[5] Oh! Wasn't it bliss indeed!

Passing by the Small Ocean

We ascended Mount Kua-ts'ang along the Evil Brook.[1] The boat moved inch by inch in the stagnant water. The sky was bullied by mountains; the river begged the rocks for mercy to let it run free. When we came to the Small Ocean,[2] all of a sudden we got a clear view. Wu Hung-chung came to see me off, bringing Jui-ju with him. We sat on straw mats outside the cabin at the prow and had a drink. The yellow-helmeted gentlemen sang a boat song for us.[3] Drooping our heads, we focused on wagering over our drinks. Presently we looked up in a startle and yelled in excitement. Only then did we know that there were colors unknown to the human world. Not knowing how those colors would be named in heaven, I can only try my best to give an approximate description by comparing them to things that exist in our world.

The semicircle of the setting sun was like rouge just emerging out of a fire. All of the mountains west of the river were either green as a parrot's plumage or black as a crow's back. Soaring above them were scarlet clouds that stretched over six thousand feet, with a large hole that let out the blue sky beyond. Their reflections in the water were like red agates spread out upon a sheet of brocade.

Now the sun was dimming. The color of the sandy beach was a mixture of gentle blue and soft white. The sand on the other bank was hardly visible in the moonlight and in the shade of the reeds. The mountains all turned the color of the rind of a ripe melon. Seven or eight patches of rosy cloud, in the shape of goose feathers or oddments of cloth, glowed like gold and litchi. These soon piled into two big clouds, which became like glittering and translucent grapes. Now layers and layers of night mountain mists, white like the bellies of fish, surged and drifted in and out of the silvery vermilion of a smelting furnace. Golden light flashed and sparkled. At this moment heaven and earth, mountains and rivers, clouds and sunshine were baking, steaming, and simmering, setting off one another. No one had any idea what kind of things would be manufactured in this huge dye-works. I suspected that its master, envious of the mirage on the sea and striving to outmaneuver Siddhartha,[4] was momentarily lifting the veil from the beauty of his colorful clouds. Perhaps he was also thinking about us—people in the boat: "Since you guys have your agitated bosoms and your straining eyes, why not lend you some creative imagination, so that you can give an account of my kaleidoscopic play of colors?"[5] Oh, what a spectacular sensation!

Now, there are only five colors in the human world.[6] When the five colors mix with one another, they will develop into no more than several tens of colors. Who could ever have imagined the existence of such fantastic, inconceivable variegation? What I have just done is only an attempt to use [the names of] things in the human world to represent the colors [in this view]. In my mind I have not yet come to a full understanding, nor had my eyes ever witnessed anything like it before. I have no choice but to find words from what my mind has comprehended and from what my eyes have seen previously, so as to make it known to others. However, what has been presented above as a rough description could never hope to approximate more than one ten-thousandth of the original scene. Oh! Without having taken a look at the wealth of heaven and earth, how could one ever know the poverty of our human world!

Shan-hsi Brook

It was unpleasant to float along in the transversel waves of the Ts'ao O River,[1] with its surface like a sheet of iron. By the time we were about to reach the Junction of Three Counties (San-chieh Chih),[2] the view of the river turned cheerful. Fishermen's fires and lamplight from the villages were in harmony with the moonshine above. Sands were shining, and mountains were still. Dogs were barking as loudly as leopards. I almost forgot that I was in a wooden boat.

At dawn we passed by Cool Breeze Ridge, where the brook joined the river, but I didn't have enough time to offer my condolences to the soul of the chaste lady.[3] Mountains were high, and banks were cramped. Verdant green intertwined with layered vermilion.[4] Rocking in the boat, I listened to a birdcall in the distance and found its soft music extremely appeasing. Every trill had its echoes from the thousands of mountain valleys around. I suspect that "between autumn and winter it would be even more exhilarating."[5]

I have no idea why Tzu-yu of our family lost his enthusiasm.[6] It was perhaps all right with Tzu-yu to make that trip to the snowy brook, but what a humiliation it must have been for Tai! Men of letters often have taken advantage of someone else's great-heartedness and have behaved in a disgraceful manner; it's really unjustified.

We passed by Picture Hill, which made a potted landscape of orchid and trumpet creepers. Thenceforth the thousands of streams, greeting one another, converged all the way into the sea, like a multitude of aristocrats dangling the jade pendants on their gowns. It was only after winding our way for a long time that a horizon of infinite expanse finally lay in front of our eyes.

The mountain town towered in the cliffs; its streets were sparsely populated toward evening. At the estuary there stood an elevated terrace like a pillar. Taking off my headcloth, I clambered up and sated myself with the cool wind there. South of the town, the Bridge of a Hundred Chang[7] spanned the brook airily, like a rainbow drinking from it.[8] Meanwhile, the brook was having its own fun beneath it, flashing like lightning and rumbling like thunder.

I had the boat moored at the end of the bridge, using the stream and the pebbles in the moonlight "to brush my teeth and to pillow my head upon," so as to have a sweet sleep.[9] The boatman, wondering why I didn't have the boat moored on the other bank, murmured to himself in disapproval of my eccentricity.

T'an Yüan-ch'un (1586–1637)

When T'an Yüan-ch'un first met his fellow townsman Chung Hsing in 1604, despite the age difference (T'an was twelve years younger), the two started a lifelong friendship and literary camaraderie. They jointly compiled the poetry anthology Destination of Poetry *(Shih kuei), divided into volumes on pre-t'ang and T'ang poetry. Upon publication in 1617, it won them immediate recognition from scholars nationwide, as well as the reputation as founders of the Ching-ling school, named after their hometown in Hu-kuang.*

The success of the anthology seems not to have had any positive impact on T'an's pursuit of an official career. He was admitted to the national university in the capital in his late forties. It was not until 1627, two years after Chung Hsing's death, that T'an passed the provincial examination with first honors, but all his subsequent attempts in the metropolitan examinations failed, and he died in an inn not far from Peking on his way to another examination.

In literary history T'an was known primarily as Chung Hsing's younger ally, and his poetry has generally been regarded as carrying to further extremes their critical arguments promoting intricacy and profundity. Ch'ien Ch'ien-i ridiculed the two, especially T'an, as "poetic monsters," not without some justification. Even at his best, as displayed in our selection here, T'an's prose, like his poetry, frequently baffles its reader (let alone its translator) with occasional incoherence and obscurity. The Sung writer Su Shih wrote two rhapsodies on his visits in different seasons to the Red Cliff along the Yangtze. T'an accepted a similar challenge in writing about his three visits to Black Dragon Pond.

First Trip to Black Dragon Pond

Most of the resorts around the White Gate[1] are on the waterfront. The Swallow Rock[2] is a nice place for sightseeing, but it is too far away. Among the lakes worthy of a visit, Mo-ch'ou[3] and Black Turtle[4] are nice, but they are outside the city wall. Among the rivers worth seeing, the Ch'in-huai[5] is nice, but too many people go there, day and night.

Now, Black Dragon Pond is inside the city, it is within easy reach by sedan chair, and, unless they really have some related business, gentlemen and ladies hardly ever go there; hence it is free from all three shortcomings of the other places. In 1612 I passed by the place and took a cursory look at it.

In 1619 my friend Mr. Mao Yüan-i[6] happened to have a veranda constructed above it. The veranda was not yet walled up. To its left there was a tower that was yet without its windows and balustrades. Both a gazebo on the waterside and a jetty paved with bricks were beginning to take shape. So he invited me to go there to have a look.

We ascended the tower; there was not much to see except the green mountain ridge in front, the verdant mounds around the pond in the back, and the deep and quiet pond itself. A neighbor's boat emerged, from aboard which Mr. Sung Hsien-ju and Mr. Fu Ju-chou looked at us, moving back and forth across the autumn scene.

Mr. Mao said, "Early autumn is nice weather. I shall ride the high tide with you, not in a boat, but on a raft." The raft, structured like a canopied tent, was being built on a wooden scaffold consisting of red-painted posts. The work was completed in three days.

Second Trip to Black Dragon Pond

The water of a pond should be clear. Woods reflected in the pond should be still. A raft should be steady. A gazebo and a veranda should be bright and open. On the Seventh Evening the River of Stars in the sky should be visible, and those who celebrate that evening should be at leisure and feel unrestrained.[1] Yet the Creator surely isn't making all those nice things for my sake, or is He?

Mr. Mao is a native of central Yüeh, so his servant boys are good at using punt-poles and oars. When we came to midstream the wind turned furious, so we could not make it to the headwaters. In a short while we arrived at the fishing dock, had the raft moored, and cast our fishhooks.

A drizzle soaked the canopy,[2] but no one wanted to go ashore. After a while it started pouring. All seven gentlemen and six courtesans stood under the canopy, each holding an umbrella, but their clothes still got wet. A windstorm started, and the pond turned wild. Scared, the courtesans rushed ashore, taking no thought of their silk gauze stockings. The gentlemen also moved up to the new veranda.

We had barely sat down when a rain flew down from the treetops. It whirled around us all the time. It splashed on the pond, but seemed to be hitting against it rather than pouring into it. Suddenly a thunderclap burst forth. The courtesans all covered their ears and tried to take refuge deep inside. Lightning and thunder came one after the other. The lightning was even more spectacular: its dazzling light shot twenty-five to thirty yards deep into the water, sucked in the light of the waves, sent it back up to the raindrops, and flashed like gold, silver, pearl, and shell for quite a while.

I doubted whether one should ever build a house by a dragon's cave in a pond and was in constant apprehension. Everything changed so suddenly that I could neither hear the laughing and talking of others nor see anything in the somber darkness; a pandemonium seemed to be close at hand. And yet some gentlemen who had gusto were enthusiastic about it. So we lit up the lanterns and started drinking, and found it somewhat easier to stand against the vital force of the wind, rain, thunder, and lightning. A courtesan suddenly arrived in the dark; only then did I realize that the vast chaos was all over the pond, or perhaps it rose right from the pond itself. On being asked about the conditions on her way here, the young lady replied that it was not like that everywhere. Wasn't that strange indeed?

The one who initiated the party was Mr. Wu Ting-fang from Tung-t'ing, and the six guests were Mr. Mao Yü-ch'ang, Mr. Hsü Wu-nien, Mr. Sung Hsien-ju, Mr. Hung K'uan, Yüan-i, and myself; plus Ting-fang, that made us a group of seven.[3]

Third Trip to Black Dragon Pond

When I made my first trip to the pond, I turned left at the Overland West Gate[1] and walked along the inside of the city wall. Reeds grew into a jungle there, but I could catch glimpses of the pond in the spaces between them. During my second trip there on the Seventh Evening, I saw on my way along the city wall first a stretch of weeping willows, then a stand of bamboos, and when the bamboos came to an end, there appeared the green reeds, extending all the way to the gardens.

Five days later Hsien-ju called for another party. Yüan-i, sitting up in his Luxuriance Tower, was not there yet. Mr. P'an Ching-sheng and Mr. Chung Hsing had arrived from Luchow. The Lin brothers and I had come southward, following a footpath from the Hua-lin Garden and Lord Hsieh's Mound.[2] We all gathered by the pond. The spirit of the pond had once made its power felt, and a shrine to worship it was built there.

The ridges of the encircling hills were undulated. From high up, beyond the tops of the trees, a waterfall fell into the pond. Cooler Hill[3] looked like a belt. At its back there was an overgrowth of shrubs where water also flowed into the deep pond through troughs from the houses around it, so the pond was as deep in winter as in summer. Although the tower was more than ten yards away, it looked as if it were standing right in the pond.

The raft could go anywhere on the pond, so it was almost like staying in a waterfront veranda. North of the pond, the lotus leaves were not yet withered and were just sending forth an autumnal sweet scent, so we gave instructions to move the raft there first. But then we fell in love with the woods across the pond and the dots of crimson walls that decorated the dark emerald, so we had the raft moored there instead.

When we first went ashore the foliage seemed impenetrable, but then we suddenly found a path and after a while we climbed atop the ridge. Beyond the hills were wilderness and quadrangular ponds, distant lakes and nearby gardens. Pointing at the view, Mr. Sung said to me, "This is indeed a hideaway fit to live in. If one could build a house at the foot of the hill, open a path leading up the hill, look down upon the clear and open pond, and take in the greenness in the front and back, one would not regret getting old here in a world of peace!" After a while Mr. Mao arrived, and he was also told the idea.

At that moment the setting sun was being trailed by the moon, and colorful clouds rose in all directions. In the crimson light the earth turned watery, and the sky glowed with various colors. At first the red light was at the waterside. Then it went over the left half of the pond. Then it rose beneath the lotus leaves, and in a short while the entire pond turned red. With the bright clouds in the background, the five colors mixed with one another in variegation.

We descended the hill and looked for the raft. By then moonlight was already waiting for us over half the pond. So we punted the raft back and had it moored under the weeping willows by the new gazebo. We looked at the moon that drifted over the waves; several tens of its golden beams reminded me of the reflection of lightning on the Seventh Evening. The drooping branches of the willows prostrated themselves in front of the moon. Oh my friends, on a bright evening like this, would you ever recall the wind and rain at our last party?

We helped one another climb up the tower, looked all around, and forgot to leave. A lantern happened to light up in the lush foliage; it was quite lovely. Someone said, "This is the lantern from a fishing boat."

Chang Tai (1597–1684?)

*Although Chang Tai lived well into the Ch'ing dynasty, he has tradition-
ally been considered a Ming writer—not unjustifiably, as he remained a loyalist to
the Ming dynasty all his life and dedicated much of his writing to memories of life
and things before the Manchu regime took over the land.*

*Much of what we know today about Chang Tai is provided by his own lively auto-
biographical sketches, including "An Epitaph for Myself" in our selection, which
offers vivid profiles of his life, aspirations, and frustrations. It suffices to say that he
was born into a rich family with a tradition for official and scholarly accomplishments. His great-grandfather Chang Yüan-pien, a Hanlin Academician and later an
instructor of the imperial heir apparent, was known for having personally helped to
get Hsü Wei out of prison. Chang Tai, however, chose not to follow the family tradition of pursuing an official career. In his youth he led a playboy's life, indulging in
extravagance and enjoying all kinds of sensual pleasures. He was known to be a
man of many talents whose range of interests and expertise included music, theater, gastronomy, tea connoisseurship, and horsemanship.*

*In his middle age Chang Tai lived through the downfall of the Ming court. For the
next two decades, while leading a hermit's life in his retreat in the mountains of
Chekiang, he witnessed the elimination of the several Southern Ming local regimes.
He wrote collections of short memoirs about the glory and sensualities of the past,
the most famous of which is* Dream Memories from the T'ao Hut, *from which
most selections here are taken. The work he took great pride in, however, was his
historical record of the Ming dynasty,* The Book in a Stone Case *(in 220* chüan*),
which he claimed required twenty-seven years to complete.*

*In a preface to his own poetry collection, Chang Tai mentioned that when he was
young he idolized Hsü Wei and, accordingly, also Hsü's promoter Yüan Hung-tao,
and tried to imitate their style in his own practice. Later he was attracted by the ris-
ing Ching-ling school and tried to write like Chung Hsing and T'an Yüan-ch'un.*

Eventually, he found that he was still closer to Hsü Wei in personality and decided to "learn to express himself" as the latter had done.

More than anyone else among both his predecessors and contemporaries, Chang Tai explored the possibilities of the hsiao-p'in, *a medium in which he found an individual voice and moved into new territories. Some of his prose pieces have been introduced to the English-reading public in elegant but unduly free renditions by Lin Yutang. One of his autobiographical sketches, the preface for his* Dream Memories, *has received a fine English translation by Stephen Owen. More recently, a few more pieces from* Dream Memories *have also appeared in anthologies compiled by Richard E. Strassberg, Victor H. Mair, and Stephen Owen.*

Selections from *Dream Memories from the T'ao Hut*

A Night Performance at Golden Hill

One day after the Mid-Autumn Festival in the second year of the Ch'ung-chen reign [1629], I passed by Chen-chiang on my way to Yen-chou. We arrived at Pei-ku [Hill] by sunset and moored our boat at the river mouth. Moonlight poured into the water as if out of a bag. The waves in the river swallowed and spat out the moonshine, and the dewy air imbibed it; it was then spurted out, whitening the sky. I was fascinated, so I had the boat moved over to Golden Hill Temple.[1] It was already the second beat of the night watches.[2] We walked through the Dragon King Shrine and entered the main hall. It was as still as death. Moonlight leaked through the woods, leaving sparse spots underneath that looked like vestiges of snow.

I called out to the boy servants to bring my stage properties, had the main hall brightly lit up, and performed the plays about General Han Shih-chung's battle at Golden Hill and along the Yangtze.[3] Gongs and drums made a deafening sound. Everyone in the temple got up to watch the performance. An old monk used the back of his hand to rub at the corneal nebula in his eyes, opened his mouth wide, and started laughing and sneezing and yawning at the same time. After a while he fixed his eyes on us, trying to figure out who we were and when and why we had come, but dared not ask any questions.

When the performance was over, it was almost dawn. We set sail and crossed the Yangtze. A monk from the mountains came down to the foot of the hill and gazed after us for a long time, as if wondering whether we were human beings, demons, or ghosts.

Plum Blossoms Bookroom

The old cottage behind Sepals Tower had collapsed. I laid a foundation about four and a half feet deep and built a large bookroom there. On its side I made an annexed alcove that looked like a screened cabinet, in which I placed a sleeping couch. I left some open space in both the front and the back of the structure. At the foot of the wall in the back I built a raised flower bed and planted three peonies, the blossoms of which, as big as the pulp of a watermelon, hung above the wall. Each year they would burst into more than three hundred flowers. In front of the terrace were two West Garrison crab apple trees.[1] When they were in bloom, we had as much as three feet of fragrant snow. The four walls in front were slightly higher. On the opposite side I constructed a stone terrace, where I placed several Lake T'ai-hu rocks[2] and planted some West Brook[3] plum [*Prunus mume*] trees, the bony trunks of which had a look of austere antiquity. Beside them a few shrubs of Yunnan camellia stood, showing off their seductive beauty. By the root of the plum trees I planted some passion-flowers [*Passiflora*], which twined round them like hairnets adorned with pearls and gemstones. Outside the windows there was a bamboo awning, topped with a canopy of thickly studded jewels. Below the steps the emerald-green grass grew more than three feet tall, set off by random plantings of begonia.

Looking through the bright windows in both the front and back, under the jeweled awning, I could watch the green of the West Garrison crab apple trees take on darker and darker shades. I used to sit or lie down inside and would allow only nice, highbred friends to enter once in a while. Out of my admiration for the Obtuse Ni's "Quiet Privacy," I also named it Cloud Forest Retreat.[4]

Drinking Tea at Pop Min's

Chou Mo-lung kept singing the praise of Min Wen-shui's tea to me.[1] In the ninth month of 1638 I arrived at the reserved capital.[2] Immediately after I got off the boat, I called upon Min Wen-shui at Peach Leaves Ferry.

It was toward sunset. Wen-shui was not at home. I waited, and when he returned, I found him to be a doddering old man. We had barely started a conversation when he suddenly got up and said, "I've forgotten my walking stick somewhere," and left again. I asked myself, "How can I leave in vain?" So I waited for him, for quite a long while.

By the time Wen-shui came back, it was quite late. He cast a sidelong glance at me, and said, "So our guest is still around, isn't he? And what is he staying here for?" I said, "I've been looking forward to meeting you for a long time. I won't leave today until I drink my fill of your tea."

Wen-shui was pleased, and he got up to personally take care of it in front of the stove. In a short while the tea was made, as fast as the coming of a sudden storm. He led me into another room with bright windows and clean furniture. There were more than a dozen kinds of Ching-hsi teapots[3] and porcelain cups produced in the Hsüan-te and Ch'eng-hua kilns,[4] all extremely exquisite. In the lamplight I took a look at the color of the tea, which did not seem to be in any way different from that in a regular cup, but its fragrance assailed my nose.

I shouted my approval and asked Wen-shui, "What kind of tea is this?" Wen-shui replied, "It's Imperial Palace tea." I took a sip and said, "Don't fool me. It was made using the same method as Palace tea, but the flavor is not the same." Trying to cover up a smile, Wen-shui said, "Does our guest know what kind of tea it is?" I took another sip and said, "Why is it so close to the Lo-chieh?"[5] Wen-shui stuck out his tongue and said, "Fabulous!"

I asked him what kind of water it was, and he told me it was from the spring at Favor Hill.[6] Again I said, "Don't fool me. If it's really from the Favor Hill spring, how could the water remain unperturbed after having made the arduous journey of more than three hundred miles?" Wen-shui said, "Now I'm going to tell you everything. To bring water from Favor Hill, you have to dredge the well first, wait for the new spring water to rise on a quiet evening, and draw it up immediately. Then you have to place pieces of mountain rocks at the bottom of the jar, and the boat carrying the water must sail and make its way here only when there is a favorable wind. In this manner, the water won't develop any bubbles. Even regular water from the Favor Hill spring is not as good as this, let alone water elsewhere!" Once again, he stuck out his tongue and said, "Fabulous!"

In the middle of our conversation Wen-shui went out. After a short while he came back with a pot, poured out a full cup from it for me, and said, "My friend, have a sip of this." I said, "The fragrance is intense, and the flavor succulent. Can this be the spring crop this year?[7] What you made earlier was the autumn pick." Wen-shui rocked with laughter and said, "I'm seventy years old, and my friend, I've never known anyone whose connoisseurship matches yours." That was how we became friends.

Viewing the Snow from the Mid-Lake Gazebo

In the twelfth month of the fifth year of the Ch'ung-chen reign [1632], I was living by West Lake. Once it snowed heavily for three days in a row. No human voice or bird cry could be heard on the lake. One day, when the last beat of the night watch was over,[1] I went aboard a small boat and, sitting by a stove in my fur coat, headed for the Mid-Lake Gazebo to catch a view of the snow there. Frosty trees stood out in the vast blankness. The sky, the clouds, the hills, and the water—all was white, overhead and beneath. The only reflections on the lake were one inky stroke for the long embankment, one dot for the gazebo, one mustard seed for my boat, and the two or three jots for people in the boat.

When I reached the gazebo, there already sat two people on a rug facing each other, and a little boy was warming up a pot of wine on the stove, which had just started boiling. They were overjoyed to see me, saying, "How could there be a guy like him on the lake?" They pulled me over to join them for a drink. I had no choice but to drain three large goblets before I bade them farewell. I asked their names and found them to be natives of Chin-ling[2] on a visit. When I got off the boat, the boatman murmured to himself, "Don't say that our young gentleman is crazy; there are people even crazier than he!"

Yao Chien-shu's Paintings

Yao Chien-shu's[1] paintings will be timeless, and so will be the man. In 1638 Chien-shu was a guest of honor at the Weis' residence.[2] At that time I made my home at Peach Leaves Ferry and exchanged friendly visits with only a couple of people, such as Min Wen-shui and Tseng Po-ch'en.[3] Chien-shu, who had never met me before, came over to see me, and the two of us immediately became the best of friends. He sojourned at my place and took care of the daily household supplies without letting me know anything about it. Whenever we had some free time, he would take me to the riverside tavern, and we would not come home until we were intoxicated. He insisted on introducing me to every single one of all the nobles, venerable elders, fellow literati, Buddhist monks, luminaries, and renowned courtesans that he knew. He had stayed at my place for ten days when an old servant came over to see him; only then did I realize that he kept a concubine at home.

Chien-shu was deep and introverted and did not like to exhibit his smartness. He was by nature a lonely person and found it very difficult to get along with others. But for reasons hard to fathom, he made great efforts to befriend me. Once we visited someone at Grace Temple, who showed us about a hundred sheets of album leaves, all works by masters of the Sung and the Yüan dynasties. Chien-shu's flashing eyes seemed to be piercing through these sheets. He sank into deep thoughts, propping himself up with his hands on the table, and looked ghastly pale. After coming home, he did two paintings modeled after Su Han-ch'en[4] for me.

A little boy is about to take a bath in a tub. He has one foot in the water and holds up the other one as if trying to get out. A palace maid squats on her heels by the tub. She holds the boy under his armpit with one hand and uses her other hand to wipe the boy's runny nose. On the other side sits another palace maid. A little boy who has just come out of the bathtub lies prone over her knees, and she is buttoning up his embroidered shirt for him.

In another painting a lady of the palace is in splendid attire, as if for some occasion. She is followed by a girl with her hair dressed up in a pair of buns. A maid stands by with a tray in her hands; on the tray are two small dishes. She looks toward the viewer. Another maid also holds onto the tray and is putting the teaspoons in order; she is all attention to her job.

Later I checked the paintings with the originals and found that he had not missed a single stroke.

Moon at Censer Peak

The summit of Censer Peak[1] stood beyond layers of mountains and winding ridges that soared and spired in entanglement. The Cliff of a Thousand *Chang*[2] stood in front, jagged and interlocked. Between the two rocks there was a gap a little less than twelve feet wide. We leaned out and looked down, and were so scared that our feet refused to move on any farther. When Wang Wen-ch'eng was a young man, he once jumped over it and was admired for his courage.[3] My uncle Erh-yün wrapped himself up in a blanket and let himself down by a rope. I was held on both sides by the arm by two woodcutters, and was pulled up from the bottom of the ravine. It was crazy indeed!

In the fourth month of 1627 I engaged myself in reading at the Celestial Tile Convent. One afternoon I went up the summit with a couple of friends to watch the sunset. A friend said, "Don't leave now. Let's wait for the moon to come out. Fine moments like this are hard to repeat. Even if we run into a tiger, it would be our destiny. Besides, tigers have their own Tao—they go down the mountain at night to look for pigs and dogs for food. I suppose they cannot be coming *up* the mountain to watch the moon rise, can they?" He surely made his point, so the four of us squatted on the Golden Tablet Rock. It was the night of the full moon that month. After the sun had gone down, the moon rose, and all the plants in the mountains looked ghostly in the moonlight, which was eerie. The mountain path was clear under the white moon, so we held on to one another and descended, using our walking sticks. We had hardly moved a few steps before we heard someone howling halfway down the mountain. It turned out to be my servant and seven or eight Buddhist monks from the mountains. They were afraid that we might have encountered a tiger and lost our way, so, holding torches and clubs in hand and carrying sheathed daggers in their boots, they came up along the mountain path and shouted to us. We responded to their call; they hurried up and helped us to get down.

The next day someone who lived on the mountainside said, "Late last night more than a hundred bandits, carrying tens of torches, went across Lord Chang's Ridge. Does anyone know where they came from?" We didn't say anything, but couldn't help laughing up our sleeves.

When Hsieh Ling-yün was opening up a road through the mountains to Lin-hai with several hundred of his attendants, Governor Wang Hsiu, who took them for bandits from the mountains, was scared and remained ill at ease until he found out that it was Ling-yün.[4] We were lucky that night not to have been tied up and sent to the governor as mountain bandits!

Liu Ching-t'ing the Storyteller

Pockmarked Liu[1] of Nanking had a dark complexion, and his face was covered with scars and swellings. "Idle and languorous by nature, he regarded his physical appearance as no more than clay and wood."[2] A great storyteller, he would tell one episode each day for the price of one tael of silver. A letter of reservation and a deposit had to be sent to him ten days in advance, and he was engaged all the time. At that time there were two popular entertainers in Nanking—none other than Wang Yüeh-sheng[3] and Pockmarked Liu.

I once listened to him tell the story "Wu Sung Knocks Out the Tiger at Ching-yang Ridge."[4] His account was quite different from that in the novel. His delineation included minute details in every possible way, and yet was well tailored and never long-winded or muddled, having weeded out all superfluities. His regular voice was already like the sound from a huge bronze bell. When he came to a critical juncture, he would shout and yell in a voice loud enough to shake the house. "Wu Sung came to the tavern to order a drink. Finding nobody at his service, he gave a raging roar that sent all the empty pitchers and jugs in the shop rumbling in echo . . ." —this is just an example of how he could draw out minute details to add color to points of repose.

Before he started, he always expected his hosts to hold their breath, sit still, and listen to him with full attention. When he was about to wag his tongue, if he ever caught sight of a servant whispering, or anyone in the audience stretching himself, yawning, or looking sleepy, he would remain silent, and no one could force him to start. Toward midnight he would dust the table clean, clip the lamp wick anew, quietly drink some tea from a white porcelain cup, and talk with ease. The tempo, volume, cadence, and modulation of his voice always fit the story, no more and no less. If all the storytellers in the world had assembled in the audience and listened to him attentively, they would have been so ashamed of themselves that they might have died from biting their tongues.

Pockmarked Liu was extremely ugly. But he was brilliant at conversation, had very expressive eyes, and wore tasteful clothing of quiet colors, so he almost matched Wang Yüeh-sheng in grace. That was why both of them commanded the highest price in the market.

West Lake on the Fifteenth Night of the Seventh Month

On the fifteenth night of the seventh month,[1] there was nothing worth seeing at West Lake except the people milling around. If you looked at people who came out on that night, you could classify them into five types.

First, there were those who came in a storied galley, bringing with them musicians playing flutes and drums. They were fully dressed up, and they ordered sumptuous meals. At a brightly lit place they enjoyed themselves in a tumult of light and sound. They were supposed to be "viewing the moon," but actually they could not see it. We could look at them.

There were also those who came in a boat or sat in a storied mansion. They were accompanied either by celebrated beauties or gentlewomen, and sometimes they also brought with them handsome boys. Laughs and sobs burst out in turn. They sat in a circle on the balcony and glanced right and left. Although they were right there under the moon, they really did not bother to give it a look. We could look at them.

There were those who came in a boat, with musicians waiting upon their pleasure, in the company of famous courtesans and Buddhist monks who had time to spare. They sipped their wine slowly and sang in a low voice, accompanied by the soft music of pipes and strings. Human voice and the sound of musical instruments set each other off. They were indeed beneath the moon, and they did view the moon, but they also wanted people to see them viewing the moon. We could look at them.

There were those who came neither in a boat nor in a carriage. They were casually dressed. After having eaten and drunk their fill, they met in groups of three to five and joined the crowd, making a lot of noise shouting and yelling at the Celebration Temple or on the Broken Bridge. They pretended to be drunk and sang tuneless songs. They looked at the moon, at those who were looking at the moon, and also at those who were not looking at the moon, but actually did not look at anything in particular. We could look at them.

There were those who came in a small boat with gauzy curtains. They sat by a clean table and a clay stove, and had water boiled in the pot to make tea; then they passed it to one another in white porcelain teacups. They came with good friends and beautiful women, and invited the moon to be their company. They either hid themselves in the shade of the trees or stayed away from the clamor on the Inner Lake. They came to view the moon, but people couldn't see how they conducted themselves while viewing the moon. Nor did they ever look at the moon with full intent. We could look at them.

When the local people in Hangchow made their trip around the lake, they usually came out around ten o'clock in the morning and returned before six in the evening. They stayed away from the moon as if from a personal enemy. On that night, however, they all came out of the city in groups, merely for the purpose of having something to brag about. They paid heavy tips to the gatekeepers.[2] Their sedan-chair carriers held torches in hand and stood in a row on the bank. As soon as they got into their boats, they instructed the boatmen to hurry for the Broken Bridge to join in the big party there. Therefore, before the second beat of the night watches, the boiling hullabaloo of human voices and music there was like that during an earthquake or in a nightmare, loud enough to make everyone deaf and mute. Boats big and small were all moored along the bank. There was nothing there to watch except the boats and the punt-poles hitting one another, and people rubbing shoulders and looking into the faces of one another. After a while their frenzy was exhausted. Government officials left after their banquets were over, yamen runners shouted to clear the way, and sedan-chair carriers yelled and scared people in the boats by saying that the city gates were closing. Lanterns and torches moved like a trail of stars, and people hurried away surrounded by their retainers. Those on the shore also hurried to go back in groups before the city gates closed. The crowd got sparser and thinner, and in a short while they were all gone.

Only then would people like us move our boats to the shore. The stone steps of the Broken Bridge had just cooled down. We placed mats on them and sat down, and invited our friends to drink to their hearts' content. Now the moon was like a newly polished mirror. The hills and the lake seemed to have just washed their faces and put on new makeup. Those who had been sipping their wine slowly and singing in a low voice came out. Those who had been hiding themselves in the shade of the trees also emerged. We greeted them and pulled them over to sit among us. Poetic friends and famous courtesans arrived on the scene. Wine cups and chopsticks were brought out. Human voices and musical instruments blended in unison. Only when the moon was fading fast and the east was gradually turning white would our guests take their leave. We set our boats adrift to find ourselves among miles of lotus flowers and to sleep soundly. There, with the fragrance assailing our nostrils, we would have sweet, sweet dreams.

Wang Yüeh-sheng

In Nanking the courtesans on Crooked Lane considered it beneath themselves to associate with those in the Vermilion Market, but Wang Yüeh-sheng, from the Vermilion Market, was definitely not to be found on Crooked Lane during the three decades of its history.[1]

Her complexion was like that of a newly blossomed autumn orchid. She was sensuous, gentle, and delicate. Her tiny ivory feet were like pink water chestnuts just out of the pond. With a reserved and noble carriage, she seldom spoke or smiled. No matter how fellow courtesans and visitors tried in many cunning ways to mock or make merry with her, they were unable to extract a beam from her. She was good at regular-script calligraphy and did paintings of orchid, bamboo, and narcissus. She also had a flair for folk songs of the Wu region, but it was not easy to get to hear her sing. Nobles and patriarchs of the southern regions always tried their best to engage her, but could hardly make her stay till the end of a banquet. Those wealthy merchants and powerful mandarins who managed to get a seat at her table for half of the evening had to send in a reservation, wrapped in a silk kerchief, a day in advance. It had to be ten taels of silver, or at least five taels; no one dared to make any lower offer. For an act of love with her, one had to send the engagement gifts one or two months in advance; otherwise, one should simply forget it for the whole year.

A fancier of tea, she was a friend of Pop Min's. Even on days of a big storm or a grand banquet, she would call upon Pop at his home and would not leave until she had sipped several pots of tea there. If she met someone whom she found attractive, she would also have a rendezvous with him at Pop's.

One day a rich merchant who lived next to Pop's had a gathering of more than a dozen courtesans from Crooked Lane. They were chatting and giggling as they sat in a circle and went on a drinking spree. Yüeh-sheng stood out on the balcony and reclined on the parapet. Shy and modest as she was, her beauty dazzled the other courtesans—so much so that they moved into another room to avoid looking at her.

Yüeh-sheng was aloof and remote like a solitary plum [*Prunus mume*] tree or a cold moon. Icy and proud by nature, she did not like to socialize with philistines. Sometimes, if she had to sit face-to-face with such a person, she would stand up and walk away as if she had not noticed him at all.

Once she was engaged by a young nobleman. Although they lived together for half a month, he failed to make her speak a word to him. One day she moved her lips haltingly. Surprised by joy, the retainers ran over to report to the young nobleman, "Yüeh-sheng is about to speak." He got very excited, as if it were an auspicious sign, and immediately ran over to have a look at her. She blushed, but did not say anything. At the young nobleman's repeated request, she just murmured, "[Let me] go home."

Crab Parties

Clams and freshwater crabs belong to the category of food in which the five flavors[1] are complete without the use of any salt or vinegar. By the tenth month, when rice and millet mature, the freshwater crab gets plump. Its bulging carapace is the size of a plate, its purple claws as big as fists, and the meat from its small legs as glossy and fatty as an arthropodal insect.

Beneath its carapace the roe or milt[2] that congeals into a lump like amber or white jade is more delicious than the eight treasures.[3]

In the tenth month my friends, my brothers, and I always held crab-eating parties. We would have such a party in the afternoon and cook crabs to eat, six for each of us. Lest they should get smelly after cooling down, we cooked them in different batches. They were accompanied by cured fat duck and cheese, amberlike liquor-saturated clams, and bok choy cooked in duck juice that looked like white jade tablets. For fruit we ate tangerines, air-dried chestnuts, and air-dried water chestnuts. For drink we had Jade-Pot Ice.[4] For a vegetable dish we had bamboo shoots from Ping-k'ang. The rice we cooked was the newly harvested Yü-hang White. We rinsed our mouths with Snow Orchid tea.[5] Looking back, it really seems like a banquet of ambrosia from the celestial kitchen, at which we ate and drank our fill. I feel ashamed just to think about it.

Lang-hsüan, Land of Enchantment

Predestination has much to do with the dreams of T'ao Hut. Once I dreamt that I was in a stone grotto hidden among masses of crags. Flowing in front was a rapid and winding stream, where water cascaded down like snow. Ancient pine trees and oddly shaped rocks stood interspersed with prized flowers. I dreamt that I sat down inside. A boy served me tea and fruit. The bookshelves were filled with books. I opened a few at random to take a cursory look, and they were mostly printed in a kind of inscription script[1] that resembled tadpoles, the footprints of birds, or thunderbolts. Yet in my dream I was able to read the script and seemed to understand everything in spite of its abstruseness.

On days when I have had nothing particular to do, I have often dreamt at night about the place. And after waking up, in an attempt to recall my dream, I have always wished to own a place with such a fine view. It would be a rock-ribbed small hill in the suburbs, with plenty of green bamboos growing on it, as if lying in ambush in the garden. There I would build an open hall facing east and west, with one study in the front and one in the back. In the back I would like to get a pebbled plot where I would plant a few pine trees from Yellow Mountain and place some rocks of strange shape to make a small canyon. In front of the hall I would plant two *so-lo* trees,[2] to take full advantage of their cool shade. On the left side I would have an annexed vacant den, where I might sit watching the foot of the hill with its jagged, toothlike crag looking as if someone had tested the sharpness of his sword on them; and I would hang a horizontal board there inscribed "One Hill." On the right side I would have three open verandas squatting on the edge of, and looking out upon, a big pond that would be clear and cool in autumn, where I might read in the dark shade of the weeping willows; and I would hang a horizontal board there inscribed "One Dale."[3] Northward along the hill, cottages and small houses next to one another would stretch in a zigzag line. There would be old trees, stratified cliffs, small streams, and secluded groves of bamboo, every joint of which would look ever so graceful. At the end of the mountain path there would be an elegant-looking cave, where I would build a burial place for myself, in preparation for the exuviation of T'ao Hut.[4] A tombstone would then be erected with the inscription, "Alas! The Grave of the T'ao Hut, Chang Chang-kung."[5] On the left of the grave there would be an open lot, about one-sixth of an acre in area, where I would build a thatched shrine to lay offerings to Buddha and also to a portrait of T'ao Hut. Monks would be invited to live there to take care of the worship services. The big pond would be about one and a half acres in area, accessible to someone with a boat along a rivulet with three or four turns. On the high mounds standing on both banks of the rivulet one might plant fruit trees such as tangerine, plum, pear, or date palm, with chrysanthemums all around. On the summit of the hill one might build a gazebo. At the western foot of the hill there would be more than three acres of fertile farmland where one might plant sorghum and rice. The front gate would face a big river, with a small tower on its wing, on top of which one might command a view of Censer Peak, Ching-t'ing,[6] and the other mountains. A gate would be constructed beneath the tower, with a horizontal board inscribed "Lang-hsüan, Land of Enchantment." Along the northern bank of the river there would be an ancient-looking stone bridge, with shrubs growing on it. There one might sit to enjoy the cool breeze or the moonlight.

An Epitaph for Myself

Chang Tai was a native of Shu [Szechwan], and T'ao Hut was his cognomen. In his youth he was a silk-stocking dandy incurably addicted to luxurious living. He was fond of fine houses, pretty maids, handsome boys, gorgeous clothes, choice food, spirited horses, bright lanterns, fireworks, the Pear Garden,[1] music, fine antiques, flowers, and birds. In addition he indulged himself in tea and fruit, and was infatuated with books and poetry.

For half of his life he had been busy with all these, but then everything turned into dream and illusion.

When he was fifty years old, his country lay shattered, his family was broken up, and he took refuge in the mountains. Nothing was left in his possession except a rickety bed, a battered desk, a damaged bronze cooking vessel, a lute out of tune, several slipcases of incomplete books, and a cracked inkslab. He began to wear plain clothes and eat simple food, and still he often failed to have regular meals. Looking back, those days of two decades ago seemed to have belonged to a previous incarnation.

Upon self-reflection, he found seven things that he could not understand.[2] In the past, though a mere civilian, he was able to rival dukes and marquises in his lifestyle; later, despite his noble pedigree, he lived no better than a beggar. The highborn and the lowbred were thus reversed. This was the first thing he could not understand. His inheritance was just below average, yet he tried to keep up with the [Master of] Golden Valley.[3] There were many shortcuts to success in the world, and yet he just missed his chance from "waiting by the stump"[4] at his retreat of Yü-ling.[5] The indigent and the wealthy were thus turned topsy-turvy. This was the second thing he could not understand. Once, as a man of letters, he set foot on the battlefield; then, being an army commander, he made his intrusion into the court of arts. The literary and the military were thus confused. This was the third thing he could not understand. Among superiors, he would not be obsequious even while attending upon the Jade Emperor,[6] but among inferiors, he would show no arrogance in the company of paupers at the almshouse. The exalted and the base were thus messed up. This was the fourth thing he could not understand. He could be so meek as to "let his face dry off by itself when spat upon,"[7] and yet he could be so audacious as to ride into the enemy's camp all alone. The lenient and the valiant were thus turned around. This was the fifth thing he could not understand. He was willing to fall behind others in pursuit of fame and gain, but when there was a stage performance or a game going on, he would rush to the front before everyone else. Matters of low and high priority were thus mistaken for each other. This was the sixth thing he could not understand. When he played chess and checkers, he did not care if he won or lost, but when he was sipping tea or tasting water, he was able to draw distinctions among various flavors. The sagacious and the foolish were thus mixed up. This was the seventh thing he could not understand.

These were the seven things incomprehensible to him. If he could not understand them himself, how could he ever expect others to? Therefore it would be perfectly all right to call him either a wealthy or a poor man, either a wise or a stupid man, either an audacious or a meek man, either a zealous or an idle man. He studied calligraphy, and he failed. He studied swordsmanship, and he failed. He studied morals and ethics, and he failed. He studied literature, and he failed. He studied Taoism, Buddhism, farming, and gardening and he failed in all. He could only let himself be called a wastrel, a good-for-nothing, a misfit, a dull-witted pedant, a sleepyhead, or a damned old fogy.

At first he adopted the style-name Tsung-tzu; then people addressed him as Master of Stone, so he assumed the style-name Shih-kung.[8] He was fond of writing books. Among the books he completed, the following were published: *The Book in a Stone Case, A Genealogy of the Chang Family, A Biography of Heroes and Martyrs, A Collection of Literary Writings from Lang-hsüan, An Explication of* The Book of Changes, *Grand Applications of* The Book of Changes, *Passageway of History, Random Notes on* The Four Books, *Dream Memories, Tinkling Bells, Interpretation of Li Ho's Poetry, Talks on the Ancients from Pleasure Garden, Ten Collections from the Servant-boy's Bag, Searching for West Lake in Dreams,* and *Prose of Ice and Snow in One Volume.*[9]

He was born at the crack of dawn on the twenty-fifth day of the eighth lunar month in 1597, during the Wan-li reign. He was the eldest son of Master Ta-t'i, counselor-delegate of the state of Lu, and his mother, T'ao, was a Lady of Suitability.[10] In his childhood he suffered from phlegmy diseases. For an entire decade he was brought up in the household of his maternal grandmother, Grand Lady Ma. His maternal grandfather was Lord of Cloud Valley, an official in Kwangtung and Kwangsi Provinces. He had a collection of raw bezoar pills, which filled up several wicker baskets. From my birth until I was sixteen, I took those pills, and I recovered my health only after I finished all of them.[11] When I was six my grandfather Master Yü-jo[12] took me to Wu-lin [Hangchow], where we ran into Master Mei-kung, who was there as a guest of the Ch'ien-t'ang magistracy, on the back of an antlered deer. He said to my grandfather, "I've been told that your grandson is good at matching antithetical couplets. Let me try it out on him." Pointing at the screen painting *Li Po Riding a Whale*, he said, "T'ai-po, riding a whale, fished for the night moon along the Stone Pit River [Ts'ai-shih Chiang]." I responded, "Mei-kung, straddling a deer, struck at the autumn wind within Coin Pond County [Ch'ien-t'ang Hsien]."[13] Mei-kung bounded to his feet and burst into laughter, saying, "How can anyone be so smart! A young friend of mine, indeed!" He wanted to encourage me to make some immortal accomplishments. How could he have anticipated that one day I would end up a total failure!

Since the year 1644 I have lived as in a daze. I am neither able to enjoy life nor to seek death. With white hair fluttering all over my head, I am still among the living and breathing. I am afraid that I will one day disappear like the morning dew or rot away like grass and trees. It therefore occurred to me that among the ancients, Wang Chi, T'ao Yüan-ming, and Hsü Wei all wrote epitaphs for themselves,[14] so I also "knitted my brows in imitation" and wrote one.[15] Once I started composing, I felt that neither myself nor my writing was good enough. Twice I put my writing brush aside and gave up. However, the piece might be worthy of being preserved, as it enumerates my errors and my idiosyncrasies.

I have already acquired an open grave for myself up Mount Chicken-head, at Hsiang-wang Hamlet.[16] My friend Li Yen-chai made an inscription for it, which reads, "Alas! Here's the coffin pit for Chang Chang-kung, author and scholar of the Ming dynasty." Liang Hung was a noble man; and the graveyard is close to that of Yao Li.[17] That is why I chose this location. Next year I will be seventy-five years old. As for the dates of my death and my burial, I have no idea yet, so I have not put it down here. Here runs the epilogue:

> A poverty-stricken Shih Ch'ung
>> contended with his Golden Valley.
> A blind Pien Ho
>> presented his jade from Ching.[18]
> An old Lien P'o
>> fought his battle at Cho-lu.[19]
> A sham of the man from the Dragon Gate
>> played his game as a historian.[20]
> A gluttonous Eastern Slope[21]
>> starved like Solitary Bamboo.[22]
> A Grand Master of the Five Black Rams—
>> would he ever be willing to sell himself?[23]
> It's all in vain to emulate T'ao Ch'ien
>> and equally futile to model after Mei Fu.[24]
> Go look for loners outside this world:
>> only they would ever know my heart.

Preface to *Searching for West Lake in Dreams*

There was something wrong with the timing of my birth. I have long been separated from West Lake—for some twenty-eight years—but everyday West Lake has emerged in my dreams, and the West Lake in my dreams has never been separated from me, not even for a single day.

In the years 1654 and 1657 I twice visited West Lake. All those lakeside villages—such as the Mansion beyond Mansions of the Shang family at the Surging Gold Gate, the Occasional Lodge of the Ch'i family, the villas of the Ch'ien and the Yü families, and my own family's Residential Garden—had been reduced to rubble.[1] What had existed in my dreams, then, turned out to be what was missing at West Lake. When I arrived at the Broken Bridge and looked around, I found that all of the supple willows and lush peach trees, and the towers and pavilions where singing and dancing had once been staged, seemed to have been inundated in a flood; fewer than one out of a hundred of these had survived.

I hurried away from the sight. I had made the trip because of West Lake, but considering what I saw there, it would have been better had I simply kept West Lake only in my dreams, which would have been left intact.

It occurred to me that my dreams were quite different from that of Li the Court Attendant.[2] The way he dreamed about Mount T'ien-mu was like dreaming about a goddess or a celebrated beauty he had never seen, so his dream was pure illusion. The way I dream about West Lake is like dreaming about home and garden and family—all in my own possession in the past, so my dreams are all reality.

I have lived as a tenant at someone else's house now for twenty-three years, but in my dreams I am still in my old residence. Today the little boy-servant who used to serve me is already white-haired, but in my dreams he remains a boy with his hair tied in a knot. I have not yet got rid of my old habits, nor am I free from my manners of yore. From now on, I shall just live in the quiet solitude of my Butterfly Hut, stay asleep or awake on my Startling Couch,[3] and do nothing but preserve my old dreams, so that the landscape of West Lake may remain untainted. When my children ask me about it, I might on occasion tell them a thing or two, though it would always sound like talking about dreams in a dream—some rigmarole, if not a nightmare.

Therefore I have written seventy-two entries of *Searching in Dreams*, to be passed on to future generations as reflections on West Lake. I am like a mountaineer who has returned from a sea voyage. When he starts praising the delicious seafood for its taste, his fellow mountaineers race with one another to come over to lick his eyes. Alas! Once the Golden Mincemeat and Jade Columns slide down beyond one's tongue, they simply vanish.[4] How could one's gluttonous craving be satisfied by a mere licking of the eyes?

The above was written by the Old Man of Ancient Sword [County][5] and Butterfly Hut, Chang Tai, on the sixteenth day of the seventh month in 1671.

Appendix A
Table of Chinese Historical Dynasties

Chou Spring and Autumn Period	770–476 B.C.E.
Warring States Period	475–221 B.C.E.
Ch'in	221–206 B.C.E.
Han	
Western Han	206 B.C.E.–C.E. 8
Hsin (Interregnum)	9–24
Eastern Han	25–220
Three Kingdoms	220–80
Western Chin	265–316
Southern Dynasties	
Eastern Chin	317–420
Sung	420–79
Ch'i	479–502
Liang	502–57
Ch'en	557–89
Sui	589–618
T'ang	618–907
Five Dynasties and Ten Kingdoms	907–60
Sung	960–1279
Northern Sung	960–1126
Southern Sung	1127–1279
Yüan (Mongol)	1279–1368
Ming	1368–1644
Ch'ing (Manchu)	1644–1911

Appendix B
Late Ming through Early Ch'ing Reign Periods

Ming Dynasty, 1368–1644

Chia-ching reign, 1522–66
    Emperor Shih-tsung (1507–67)
Lung-ch'ing reign, 1567–72
    Emperor Mu-tsung (1537–72)
Wan-li reign, 1573–1620
    Emperor Shen-tsung (1563–1620)
T'ai-ch'ang reign, 1620
    Emperor Kuang-tsung (1582–1620)
T'ien-ch'i reign, 1621–27
    Emperor Hsi-tsung (1605–27)
Ch'ung-chen reign, 1628–44
    Emperor Ssu-tsung (1611–44)

Southern Ming (local governments), 1644–62

Hung-kuang reign (Nanking), 1644–45
    Chu Yu-sung, Prince of Fu (Emperor An-tsung, 1607–46)
Lung-wu reign (Foochow), 1645–46
    Chu Yü-chien, Prince of T'ang (Emperor Shao-tsung, 1602–46)

Lu regency (Chekiang, Fukien), 1645–53
  Chu I-hai, Prince of Lu (1618–62)
Shao-wu reign (Canton), 1646–47
  Chu Yü-yüeh, Prince of T'ang (d. 1647)
Yung-li reign (Kwangtung, Kwangsi, Yunnan), 1646–62
  Chu Yu-lang, Prince of Kuei (1623–62)

Ch'ing Dynasty (Manchu), 1644–1911

Shun-chih reign, 1644–61
  Emperor Shih-tsu (1638–61)
K'ang-hsi reign, 1662–1722
  Emperor Sheng-tsu (1654–1722)

Notes

Hsiao-p'in of the Late Ming: An Introduction

1. For most English-language references, see the Bibliography. Where necessary, page and volume numbering is provided in brackets in text.

2. For the convenience of the Western reader, I have used as an approximate to the Chinese term *hsiao-p'in* the word "vignette," of Old French origin, which has been defined as "a short literary sketch chiefly descriptive and characterized usually by delicacy, wit, and subtlety" (*Webster's Third New International Dictionary*, 1981).

3. For Chinese-language references, see the Bibliography. Where necessary, page and section (*chüan*) numbers are given in brackets in the text.

4. The Six Dynasties (222–589) traditionally referred to the Wu, Eastern Chin, and successive southern dynasties of Sung, Ch'i, Liang, and Ch'en, for all of which Chien-k'ang (modern Nanking) was the capital city.

5. For an English translation of this piece, see Lin Yutang, *Translations from the Chinese*, pp. 98–99. A more recent rendition is in Strassberg, pp. 63–66.

6. For an English translation of three passages from *A Commentary on the Water Classic*, see Strassberg, pp. 77–90.

7. *Shih-shuo hsin-yü* was written by Liu I-ch'ing (403–44), with supplementary annotations by Liu Chün (462–521). There is an English translation by Richard B. Mather.

8. See Wang's preface to a new edition of the *Shih-shuo hsin-yü*, in Shih Che-ts'un, ed., *Wan-Ming erh-shih-chia hsiao-p'in*, pp. 303–4.

9. For another English translation, see Strassberg, pp. 192–93.

10. See Yüan's letter to Ts'ai Yüan-lü in *K'o-hsüeh-chai chi*, III, p. 1385.

11. *Chüan* often is translated into English as "volume." Although the terms match etymologically (both originally meant "a roll of writing"), one must remember that *chüan* refers to a section of a book, sometimes only a page or two in length.

12. See the Introduction to Lu Jun-hsiang, p. 6; also Chih-p'ing Chou, *Yüan Hung-tao and the Kung-an School*, p. 91, p. 139 n. 2.

13. See Liu I-ching, IV:30, p. 119; IV:43, p. 124; IV:45, p. 125; IV:50; p. 127.

14. To give just a few examples of single-author works, there were Ch'en Chi-ju's *Wan-hsiang-t'ang hsiao-p'in* (Vignettes from the Hall of Evening Fragrance), Wang Ssu-jen's *Wen-fan hsiao-p'in* (Vignettes as literary meals), and Ch'en Jen-hsi's

(1579–1634) *Wu-meng-yüan chi hsiao-p'in* (A collection of vignettes from the dream-less garden), all titled by the authors themselves. Multiauthor collections of vignettes by the Sung writers Su Shih and Huang T'ing-chien bearing the term *hsiao-p'in* in the title were published during the Wan-li reign, and the extremely popular anthology *Huang Ming shih-liu-chia hsiao-p'in* (Vignettes by sixteen authors of the imperial Ming), compiled by Lu Yün-lung, was printed in 1633. For a list of such works from the late Ming and early Ch'ing periods see Ch'en Wan-i, pp. 26–27.

15. *Ch'en Mei-kung ch'üan-chi*, pp. 112–13.

16. *I-yüan chih-yen chiao chu*, III: 4, p. 102.

17. *Cheng-ch'uan hsien-sheng chi*, I, p. 21. Here Kuei cites the opening lines from the poem "Bantering Chang Chi" by the famous T'ang writer Han Yü (768–824).

18. See Ch'ien Ch'ien-i's short biography of Kuei Yu-kuang, included in the Appendices of *Cheng-ch'uan hsien-sheng chi*, II, p. 977.

19. See Huang K'ai-hua; also "New Light on Ming China: An Interview with Richard von Glahn," *ISOP Intercom* (University of California, Los Angeles), vol. 15, no. 8 (1 February 1993).

20. See Ch'ien's short biography of Kuei, in *Cheng-ch'uan hsien-sheng chi*, II, pp. 977–78.

21. For a short biography of Chang Tai by Fang Chao-ying see Hummel, I, pp. 53–54. Of the several histories of Chinese literature written in English, the only one that refers briefly to Chang Tai and the *hsiao-p'in wen* is that by Lai Ming (pp. 3, 320); it also includes a translation of Chang Tai's "Harvest Moon on West Lake" (pp. 320–22). More than anyone else, Lin Yutang introduced the *hsiao-p'in*—including a few by Chang Tai, in his elegant but frequently unduly free rendition (often more adaptation than translation)—to the English reader; but Lin's excellent pioneering work is largely ignored today by Western sinologists and has had little, if any, response in serious critical writings. The only critical reading of Chang Tai is found in Stephen Owen's *Remembrances* (pp. 134–41), which provides a fine translation of one of Chang Tai's autobiographical sketches, his own preface to *Dream Memories from the T'ao Hut*.

22. Other examples are Wang I-sun and Chiang Chieh. See Chia-ying Yeh Chao, "On Wang I-sun and His *Yun-wu Tz'u*," *Harvard-Yenching Journal of Asian Studies* 40.1 (1980): pp. 55–91; Yang Ye, "Chiang Chieh and His *Tz'u* Poetry," *Journal of Sung-Yüan Studies* 24 (1994), pp. 21–55.

23. Many of these publications are included in "Primary Texts" section of the Bibliography. Among the hundreds of new *hsiao-p'in* anthologies published in the last decade, I have found the following three most useful: T'ang Kao-ts'ai, Hu I-ch'eng, and Hsia Hsien-ch'un 1995. Hsia's anthology is of a remarkably higher academic quality. Two commendable studies of individual *hsiao-p'in* authors are Jen Fang-ch'iu and Hsia Hsien-ch'un 1989.

24. I would just mention a few here. Among the more general studies, I recommend Ch'en Shao-t'ang and Ch'en Wan-i; and, among studies of individual authors, Liang I-ch'eng on Hsü Wei; and T'ien Su-lan, Yang Te-pen, and Yüan Nai-ling on Yüan Hung-tao.

25. *Yale French Studies*, no. 64 (1983), edited by Gérard Defaux and entitled *Montaigne: Essays in Reading*, made an exception by devoting itself to a study of the great

author of *essais*, including two delightfully thoughtful pieces by Tzvetan Todorov and Jean Starobinski.

26. See Martine Vallette-Hémery, *Nuages et pierre: Yuan Hongdao* (Paris: Publications Orientalistes de France, 1982), *Yuan Hongdao [Hung-tao] (1568–1610): Théorie et pratique littéraires* (Paris: Collège de France, *Mémoires de l'Institut des Hautes Études Chinoises* 18, 1982).

Kuei Yu-kuang

Foreword to "Reflections on *The Book of Documents*"

1. The Southern Capital was the city of Nanking, so called to distinguish it from the Northern Capital of Kaifeng (1368) and eventually Peking (1421).

2. *The Book of Documents* is the earliest extant collection of historical documents, political decrees, and government regulations of the ancient Shang and Chou dynasties, canonized during the Han dynasty as one of the six Confucian scriptures.

3. Citation from an essay by the Sung writer Su Shih, "A Note on Wen Yu-k'o's Painting of the Tall Bamboos in the Yün-tang Valley." Su also used a variation of the metaphor in his famous poem "The Hundred-Step Waterfall."

Inscription on the Wall of the Wild Crane Belvedere

1. Liu Kuo (cognomen Taoist of Lung-chou, 1154–1206), a song-lyric poet of the Southern Sung.

The Craggy Gazebo

1. *Chuang-tzu* is an ancient classic attributed to Chuang Chou (369?–286? B.C.E.), respectfully addressed as Master Chuang, or Chuang-tzu, a thinker of the Warring States period.

2. Respectfully addressed as Lao-tzu (real name Li Erh, 604?–531? B.C.E.), he was a legendary thinker and honored as the founder of Taoism. His sayings are found in the classic *Tao te ching*.

3. A picul (*shih*, or "stone") is about 2.75 bushels, or roughly 22 gallons.

The Hsiang-chi Belvedere

1. Kuei Tao-lung, a distant ancestor of the author's, once lived at a place called Hsiang-chi Creek in T'ai-ts'ang County, Kiangsu. The belvedere was named in his memory, and the author sometimes used "Master Hsiang-chi" for his cognomen.

2. When a boy was old enough to start learning (at age five or six), his hair was tied up in a knot on top of his head.

3. A court tablet, rectangular in shape and usually made of ivory, jade, or bamboo slips, was held by an official when he went to the imperial court.

4. The author's maternal great-grandfather was the famous Ming painter Hsia Ch'ang (1388–1470), particularly known for his paintings of the bamboo.

5. The story about Widow Ch'ing of Shu (Szechwan), who made a fortune with her mine of cinnabar (needed for making Taoist longevity pills), was told in Ssu-ma Ch'ien's *Historical Records* ("The Biography of the Moneymakers").

6. During the period of the Three Kingdoms, Ts'ao Ts'ao (155–220) was the ruler of Wei, and Liu Pei (161–223) was the ruler of Shu. Liu Pei went to Lung-chung three times to visit the recluse Chu-ko Liang (181–234), who finally agreed to serve under Liu, and was appointed prime minister of Shu.

7. The reference to a frog (who has no idea how big the world is) down in the well is from a fable in the "Autumn Waters" chapter in the classic *Chuang-tzu*. The following passage is a postscript.

Lu Shu-sheng

Inkslab Den

1. The phrase "superfluous thing" alludes to an anecdote in the classic *A New Account of Tales of the World* (I, 44). Wang Ch'en called upon his cousin Wang Kung on the latter's return from a trip to the southeast, and saw him sitting on a summer mat (made of interwoven split bamboo). Thinking that Kung must have obtained a few of those during his trip, Ch'en asked for one. Without a word, Kung had the mat sent over, even though it was the only one in his possession. Later, Ch'en heard about it and was stunned. He told Kung, "I asked you for one because I thought you had quite a few." Kung answered, "You don't know me. I am a person who doesn't own any superfluous thing."

2. Considered one of the best inkslabs by Chinese calligraphers since the T'ang dynasty, the Tuan inkslab was named after Tuan-chou (Chao-ch'ing in modern times), Kwangtung, the place of its production.

3. The She inkslab, also considered one of the best since the T'ang, was named after She-chou, Anhwei, the place of its production.

4. Men of letters of the Sung dynasty. Ou-yang Hsiu was a leading poet and prose master. Ts'ai Hsiang (1012–67) was one of the Four Masters of Calligraphy of the Sung. Hung Kuo (1117–84) was a famous collector and epigraphist. The inkstone used to make the She inkslab is found at Dragon-Tail Hill in She-chou, so the She inkslab is sometimes also called the Dragon-Tail inkslab.

5. This alludes to an anecdote from *History of the Chin* (Chin-shu) about Wang Hsien-chih (344–86), the son of Wang Hsi-chih and a renowned calligrapher himself. One night, while Hsien-chih was lying on his bed, a couple of burglars entered his room and began taking everything. After a while Hsien-chih calmly said, "Thieves, the black felt blanket is an old relic of my family. You had better put it down." The burglars were startled and ran away. The phrase "black felt blanket" has thenceforth referred to a keepsake or relic.

Bitter Bamboo

1. In the Ming dynasty, Chiang-nan (lit., "South of the River") referred to the Yang-tze River delta, which included southern Kiangsu and parts of Chekiang and Anhwei.

A Trip to Wei Village

1. Ts'ung-wen Gate was one of the city gates of Peking.

2. Wang Wei (701–61), the great T'ang poet and painter, served as assistant director of the Department of State Affairs. The cited line is from one of his court poems
in heptasyllabic regulated verse, which tells about a spring outing in the rain.

3. T'ao Yüan-ming, alias T'ao Ch'ien (365–427), was a great poet of the Southern
Dynasties (Eastern Chin and Sung). Here the author jokingly called the cool wind
"T'ao Yüan-ming's old friend" in an allusion to what T'ao once wrote in a letter to
his sons: "I often say that during the fifth and sixth [lunar] months, while lying
down under the northern windows, whenever a cool wind arises, I would consider
myself someone from remote antiquity."

A Short Note about My Six Attendants in Retirement

1. The kingdoms of Yen and Chao of the period of Warring States were located in
the region of northern China that is now Hopei and part of Shansi.

2. The Five Sacred Mountains are T'ai-shan in Shantung, Heng-shan in Hunan,
Hua-shan in Shansi, Heng-shan in Hopei, and Sung-shan in Honan, representing
respectively the mountain gods of the east, south, west, north, and center. Emperors
of different dynasties since the Han had made sacrifices to these mountains, and
they were sanctified by Emperor T'ai-tsu of the Ming.

3. Tsung Ping (375–443) was a painter of the Southern Dynasties (Sung). He had
traveled widely in his life, and when he was too old to do so, he painted on walls the
landscapes he had seen, saying, "I now clear my mind to watch the Tao, and make
my recumbent travels."

4. Two anecdotes are used here in allusion. The former is from the "T'an Kung"
section in the *The Book of Rites*. When Confucius's pet dog died, the Master asked his
disciple Tzu-kung to have it buried, saying, "I have heard that one does not throw
away worn-out draperies so that they may be used to bury one's horse, that one does
not throw away worn-out canopies so that they may be used to bury one's dog." The
latter is from the biography of Wei Hsiung in *History of the Northern Dynasties* (Pei-
shih). Wei Hsiung paid a visit to a governor. On departure, the governor gave Hsiung
his own horse with all its fancy trappings. Hsiung declined, saying, "In the old days
one would not throw away dropped hairpins and old shoes, because one would hate
to go out wearing them but to come back without them. Although I cannot match
those good people of the past in my behavior, nor would I like to discard old things
and pick up new ones." So he went home on his own old horse. Both stories involve
tenderness for things that have been in one's possession for a long time.

Inscription on Two Paintings in My Collection

1. "Fine brushwork" (*kung-pi*) is a genre of traditional Chinese painting characterized by close attention to detail.

2. Han Huang and his student Tai Sung were T'ang masters who specialized in
painting cattle.

3. Han Yü was a great prose writer, poet, and statesman. His "Note on a Painting" is a frequently anthologized prose piece.

Inscription on a Portrait of Tung-p'o Wearing Bamboo Hat and Clogs

1. The painting for which this piece was written, long since lost, was said to be a self-portrait by Su Shih (cognomen Tung-p'o Chü-shih, or Lay Buddhist of Eastern Slope) during his exile. This one was probably an imitation. The bamboo hat is one with a shaped crown and brim, made of interwoven thin strips of bamboo stem, habitually worn by farmers and fishermen.

Hsü Wei

To Ma Ts'e-chih

Ma Ts'e-chih was a student of Hsü. This short note was probably written in late 1576, when the author was serving as a private secretary to fellow townsman and former classmate Wu Tui, the Grand Coordinator of Hsüan-fu Prefecture on the northern frontier.

1. The heatable brick bed (k'ang), which serves as a desk as well as a bed, is still widely used in northern China today.

2. Water chestnuts and bamboo shoots are delicacies generally available only in the Chiang-nan area.

Another Colophon

This is the second of two colophons inscribed on the same scroll. A model script (t'ieh) is the copy of a text by a calligraphy master that is used by students as a model for imitation. "The Seventeenth" is a famous "cursive style" model calligraphic script by Wang Hsi-chih. The holograph was a personal letter that started with the characters shih ch'i jih (the seventeenth day), hence the title. The Court of the Imperial Stud was principally responsible for the management of state horse pasturage throughout the empire and for the maintenance of related vehicles and gear.

A Dream

1. Lit., "a sardonic grin."

Li Chih

Three Fools

1. Li Pai-yao (565–648) was a famous historian of the T'ang dynasty.

In Praise of Liu Hsieh

1. "Learner of the Tao" (*Tao-hsüeh*) referred to those who engaged themselves in the study of what has been frequently translated in a narrow sense into English as Neo-Confucianism, the school of learning that assimilated Taoism and Buddhism in a reexamination of Confucianism, established by the Sung thinkers Chou Tun-i (1017–73), the brothers Ch'eng I (1032–85) and Ch'eng Hao (1033–1107), and Chu Hsi (1130–1200). Their followers were often accused of affectation and hypocrisy. The "three cardinal guides" (sovereign guides subject, father guides son, and husband guides wife) and "five constant virtues" (benevolence, righteousness, propriety, wisdom, and trustworthiness) were established by Confucians of the Han dynasty. "Human relationship" (*jen-lun*) refers to the Confucian ethics regarding the relationships between sovereign and subject, father and son, husband and wife, elder and younger siblings, and friends.

2. Confucius is the Latinized form of K'ung-fu-tzu, or Master K'ung, traditionally the respectful form of address for the great Chinese thinker K'ung Ch'iu (styled Chung-ni, 551–479 B.C.E.).

3. Liu Hsieh, who received the degree of Metropolitan Graduate during the Lung-ch'ing reign, was once appointed magistrate of Yü-ch'ing County, Kiangsi.

4. These two anonymous lines (pentasyllabic in the original), found on the wall of a wayside inn in Szechwan, were cited in a volume of "remarks on poetry" (*shih-hua*) by the Sung author T'ang Keng (1070–1120). They were popularized through Chu Hsi's quotation.

5. Hsi-huang, or Fu-hsi, a legendary ruler in ancient China, was one of the Three Sovereigns (San Huang) glorified by Confucius as early sages.

Inscription on a Portrait of Confucius at the Iris Buddhist Shrine

1. All quotations are from the Confucian classics *The Analects* (the sayings of Confucius and his disciples) and *Mencius* (*Meng-tzu*; the sayings of Mencius), which were among the Four Books canonized by Chu Hsi.

2. The Iris Buddhist Shrine was a lodge built by the author's friends to be used as a private chapel for his Buddhist studies as well as for his residence. It was located by the Dragon Pool northeast of the city of Ma-ch'eng.

Essay: On the Mind of a Child

This more formal essay is included here along with *hsiao-p'in* by Li Chih because of its significance among his works.

1. *The Western Chamber* is a famous play about a romantic love affair written by the playwright Wang Shih-fu of the Yüan dynasty.

2. Yen Chün, a thinker of the T'ai-chou school and contemporary of the author's, is known by his "style" name, Mountain Farmer. Some have regarded it as a cognomen of Li Chih himself.

3. This is from a proverb: "When a short person watches a stage performance, he can only echo the comments of others [because he cannot see by himself]."

4. *The Old Poems* (Ku shih) are a group of nineteen poems, written in pentasyllabic verse during the late second century. *The Anthology* refers to the poems included in the *Wen hsüan* (An anthology of literature), compiled by Hsiao T'ung (501–31), Prince Chao-ming of the Liang dynasty. Both have been considered models par excellence for later poets.

5. Here the author ridicules the retrogressive concepts of literary history promoted by contemporary neoclassicists such as the Later Seven Masters, who maintained that one should model only after the pre-Ch'in works in prose writing, and only up to the High T'ang works in poetry composition.

6. The "new forms" refer to the several forms of "regulated verse" (*lü-shih*) that began to flourish in the T'ang dynasty.

7. *Ch'uan-ch'i* (lit., "transmission of the strange") is a literary term whose definition has varied in different ages. Here it probably refers to the short classical prose fiction that was popular during the late T'ang dynasty. It was also used for drama in the Ming dynasty.

8. *Yüan-pen* is a generic name for the early drama during the Jurchen Chin reign (1115–1234) in northern China.

9. *Tsa-chü* is a generic name for the drama of the Mongol Yüan dynasty.

10. *Water Margin* is a novel, attributed to Shih Nai-an (1296?–1370?), that tells the story of a band of robbers.

11. The Six Classics are *The Book of Songs* (Shih ching), *The Book of Documents, The Book of Rites, The Book of Music* (Yüeh ching; no longer extant), *The Book of Changes* (I ching) and *The Spring and Autumn Annals* (Ch'un ch'iu), canonized as Confucian scriptures during the Han dynasty.

T'u Lung

A Letter in Reply to Li Wei-yin

1. During the Han dynasty the Orchid Terrace (Lan-t'ai) was the Imperial Archives; by the T'ang dynasty the name was used for the Department of Palace Library, also known as the Orchid Department (Lan-sheng). In later usage the term often referred to one of the departments of the central government. Here it refers to the Ministry of Rites, where the author served.

2. The Ch'in-huai River, a tributary of the Yangtze in southeastern Kiangsu, flows through the city of Nanking.

3. The "Clear Void" is a Taoist term that refers to a pure mind in harmony with the Tao, or the Way of Nature.

4. Tsou Yüan-piao (1551–1624) was an official and philosopher. He won the degree of Metropolitan Graduate in the same year as T'u Long (1577).

5. Traditionally, "Sagacious Sovereign" referred to the ruler in power.

6. Moling was an ancient county in Kiangsu near Nanking. Here it refers to Nanking. In 1584 Tsou Yüan-piao was demoted to serve in the Ministry of Justice there.

7. In classical literary usage, the term "beautiful one" was often used for a person one admired, especially an ideal Confucian personality.

To a Friend, while Staying in the Capital

1. Here Yen refers to the capital, Peking. The capital of the ancient dukedom (since the 11th cent. B.C.E.) and later the kingdom (332–221 B.C.E.) of Yen was located in what is now the southwestern part of Peking.

2. Ch'ang-an (modern Sian or Hsi-an) was the capital of many dynasties. Here it is a synonym for the capital, i.e., Peking.

To a Friend, after Coming Home in Retirement

1. The Gate of Splendor was one of the gates of the city of Ch'ang-an, the capital city during the T'ang dynasty. Here it refers to one of the city gates of Peking.

2. Built in 644 at the foot of Mount Li-shan in Ling-t'ung County near Ch'ang-an, the Hua-ch'ing Palace, which housed a hot spring, became the famous setting of the amorous relationship between the T'ang emperor Hsüan-tsung (r. 712–55) and his concubine Yang Yü-huan. It was burned down in the rebellion that started in 755. Here it refers to the imperial palace in general.

3. O-p'ang Palace was built by order of the First Emperor of the Ch'in empire (r. 221–210 B.C.E.). It was never completed, and the front part of the palace, built in 221 B.C.E., was destroyed with the fall of the empire in the year 206 B.C.E. The Mi-lou (lit., "Tower To Get Lost In") was a labyrinth constructed during the reign of the Sui emperor Yang-ti (605–17), who indulged himself in all kinds of sensual pleasures inside.

4. The ancient kingdoms of Wu and Yüeh were located in southeastern China (mainly modern Kiangsu and Chekiang).

Ch'en Chi-ju

Trips to See Peach in Bloom

1. The Birthday of the Flowers was celebrated on the second, twelfth, or fifteenth day (varying geographically) of the second month in the Chinese lunar calendar. Judging from the context, here it refers to the twelfth day.

2. "Red rain" refers to the falling of flower petals caused by the activity of the visitors.

3. In the Ming, an administrator (ch'ang-shih) was the chief executive official in a princely establishment. Here it probably refers to Yüan Tsung-tao, who served as a secretary to the heir apparent.

4. This Mr. T'ien (lit., "Mr. Farmer") may be the same old man whose property the author and his friends trespassed on the previous day.

5. "Guessing the fist" (ts'ai ch'üan) was a finger-guessing game traditionally played at drinking parties for a wager of who should drink more.

6. The ending here refers to the famous poem "Peach Blossom Fountain" and its prose preface written by the poet and recluse T'ao Yüan-ming, in which he described how a fisherman coincidentally came to a secluded mountain valley and was told by local residents that they had fled from upheavals during the Ch'in dynasty.

"Inquiring about the ferry," a phrase quoted from the prose preface, has become a synonym for adventure or exploration. "Gentleman Summoned to Office" (Cheng-chün) was a common unofficial reference to one who was nominated by local authorities for possible official appointment, regardless of whether he accepted. T'ao served in several insignificant positions on assignments from local authorities. The author himself, who was repeatedly recommended to the court but never accepted any appointment, was often addressed by his friends by the same title.

Inscription on Wang Chung-tsun's *A History of Flowers*

1. Confucianism, Taoism, and Buddhism.

2. A "low cap" (in contrast to the peaked cap worn by officials) was one for commoners, according to historical records of the T'ang dynasty. The phrase "long-bearded" comes from Han Yü's "Poem Sent to Lu T'ung": "I have a long-bearded servant who leaves his hair in a tousle / And a barefooted old maid who has no more teeth left." Both are used here as epithets for servants.

3. The friend was poking fun at the author with a pun here. Traditional Chinese astrologers referred to one's love experience as "the peach flower in destiny." "Brow Taoist" refers to the author's cognomen, Mei-kung, or Master Brow.

4. The author's retort involves another astrological concept: when the Post-Horse Star is over someone's destiny, he or she would be doomed to make long journeys or to relocate.

5. When Liu Pei was still subordinate to Ts'ao Ts'ao, who later became his rival, he lived in seclusion and spent his time planting vegetables and "watering his garden," so as to hide his ambitions from the latter, who suspected him to be a future rival.

6. "Those who fly and eat meat" are power-hungry officials. In the history classic *Tso's Commentary* (Tso chuan), Ts'ao Mei, a recluse, came to the rescue of the duke of Lu when the army of the Ch'i dukedom invaded Lu in the year 684. He told the duke, "Those who eat meat are vulgar, short-sighted people not worth counseling." The term "meat eater" has since become an epithet for government officials.

A Colophon to *A History of Flowers*

1. The "twenty-one histories" refers to the official dynastic histories from Ssu-ma Ch'ien's *Historical Records* down to *The History of the Yüan*. During the reign of Emperor Kao-tsung of the Manchu dynasty, three more were added to the list, and afterward the phrase "twenty-four histories" stood for all of the official dynastic histories.

A Colophon to *A Profile of Yao P'ing-chung*

Yao P'ing-chung was a military general during the Northern Sung dynasty who led, beginning at the age of eighteen, many victorious battles against invading troops from the northwestern state of the Western Hsia. In 1126, after an unsuccessful night raid against the troops of the northeastern state of the Jurchen Chin, he disappeared into the Blue Castle Mountains (Ch'ing-ch'eng-shan) in Szechwan and remained there in hiding until half a century later, when he was a senile person in his eighties. *A Profile of Yao P'ing-chung* was written by the Southern Sung poet and writer Lu Yu (1125–1210) and included by Ch'en Chi-ju in his anthology *A Selection of Extra-Canonical Classical Prose* (Ku-wen p'in-wai lu).

1. Lady Li was a favorite consort of the Martial Emperor of the Han (r. 140–87 B.C.E.). General Ma was Ma Yüan (14 B.C.E.–C.E. 49), who in the year of C.E. 41 was given the title Waves-Riding General (Fu-po Chiang-chün) and enfeoffed as a marquis for his military accomplishments. The author seems to have made a mistake here, as Lady Li is known to have died a young woman.

2. Hsi-tzu (alias Hsi Shih), a famous beauty of the fifth century B.C.E., was a native of the state of Yüeh. She agreed to seduce King Fu-ch'ai (r. 493–473 B.C.E.) of the Wu kingdom and became his favorite consort. After the elimination of the Wu kingdom she is said to have gone into seclusion. In pre-Ch'in usage the term "Five Lakes" refers to Lake T'ai-hu in southern Kiangsu.

3. The legendary dragon (*lung*) was regarded as divine and ruler of the sea.

Selections from *Privacies in the Mountains*

1

1. The night was divided into five periods of approximately two hours each. At the beginning of each period the official night watchman would beat the watch from the drum tower or in the streets.

2. Smaller Mount K'un-shan, located in northwest Sung-chiang Prefecture in Kiangsu, is so called to distinguish it from Horse Saddle Hill (see Kuei Yu-kuang's "Inscription on the Wall of the Wild Crane Belvedere"), which is also called Mount K'un-shan, in nearby K'un-shan County.

3. "Plum rain" refers to the season of intermittent rains and drizzles, usually in April and May, in the middle and lower reaches of the Yangtze.

3

1. Many popular Chinese ornamental plants have no common English names. Both the *mei-hua* (*Prunus mume*) and *li-hua* (*Prunus salicina*) fall under the English word "plum," a general term for any species of the genus *Prunus*. The American (*Prunus americana*) and European (*Prunus domestica*) species of *Prunus* are close to the *li-hua*, but quite different from the *mei-hua* referred to here, which is the earliest to flower. I have rendered it as "early plum" or attached its Latin name in brackets to mark the difference.

2. A "versifying soul" is a poet.

4

1. Mulberry leaves are fed to silkworms.

7

1. The "plum wind" is that in the humid season of the "plum rain."

2. The water-shield (*Brasenia schreberi*) is an aquatic plant, the leaves and tender stems of which are considered a delicacy. The best are from West Lake in Hangchow.

The perch (*Lateolabrax japonicus*) is a prized fish found in brackish water near the coast. The reference to these two delicacies carries an allusion to an anecdote in *A New Account of Tales of the World* (VII, 10). During the Chin dynasty Chang Han, a native of Wu, was serving under Prince Ch'i in the capital of Loyang. One day when the autumn wind arose, Chang suddenly missed the "water-shield soup" and "minced perch" of Chiang-nan. He said, "We are supposed to enjoy ourselves in life. How could anyone get trapped in official duties and stay thousands of miles away from home in search of fame and rank?" Soon afterward he left for home.

8

1. The Peaks are the several hills (Mount She-shan, etc.) located in Sung-chiang Prefecture, Kiangsu. Lake Mao, also known as the Three Maos (upper, middle, and lower), which lay west of Sung-chiang, has vanished today due to silting.

2. Ching-k'ou was an ancient city sited at what is now Chen-chiang, Kiangsu, at the crossing of the Grand Canal and the Yangtze. Ch'ien-t'ang is an old name for Hangchow. The Chiang-nan section of the Grand Canal leads from Chen-chiang all the way to Hangchow.

Yüan Tsung-tao

Little Western Paradise

1. Built in 1189–92, Lu-kou Bridge spans the Yung-ting River in the southwestern suburbs of Peking.

2. "Western Paradise" originally referred to the Buddhist Pure Land in the "west," i.e., India. "Little Western Paradise" was a name given to one of the peaks in the Stone Scriptures Hills (Shih-ching-shan) in the southwestern suburbs of Peking.

3. The *kung* originally was an ancient bronze drinking vessel, usually with a lid in the shape of an animal's head. Here it probably just refers to a large goblet.

A Trip to Sukhāvatī Temple

1. Sukhāvatī Temple (Chi-lo Ssu), outside the Western City Gate of Peking, was a popular tourist spot during the Ming dynasty. Sukhāvatī is the Sanskrit term for "pure land" or "paradise."

2. Su Embankment, about 1.7 miles in length, which spans West Lake in Hang-chow and divides it into the Inner Lake and the Outer Lake, was built when the great Sung poet Su Shih was governor of Hangchow and is so called in his memory. Along the embankment are the famous Six Bridges, which have been popular tourist spots. Ch'ien-t'ang County was the seat of the governments of Chekiang Province and Hangchow Prefecture during the Ming dynasty.

A Trip to Yüeh-yang

1. Stonehead (Shih-shou) is a county in southern Hupei adjacent to Hunan. Yüeh-yang is a city on the southern bank of the Yangtze in northeast Hunan. In the

old days Chinese women wore their hair in a bun or coil in the shape of a conch shell.

2. In the Ming dynasty a Cultivated Talent (Hsiu-ts'ai) was one who passed the civil service examination at the county level and was admitted to the prefectural school.

3. "Liu the Cultivated Talent" refers to Liu I, the title hero of a T'ang short story (ch'uan-ch'i) by Li Ch'ao-wei, "A Biography of Liu I," which tells about Liu's adventure in the underwater palace of the dragons.

Selections from *Miscellanea*

2

1. There are more rivers and lakes in south China than in the north, hence the stereotype.

2. An allusion to a passage in *Chuang-tzu* (VIII, "Double Toes"): "A duck has short legs, but if we stretch them, it will be unhappy. A crane has long legs, but if we cut them short, it will be sad."

5

1. Po Chü-yi (772–846) is arguably the best-known Chinese poet internationally. He was extremely popular in Korea and Japan even in his lifetime. According to his biography in the official *History of the T'ang*, every time he composed some new poems, handwritten copies were sold at a high price. His poems were made into songs that singing girls all tried to learn. In Korea merchants from China who presented new poems by Po to the prime minister received a piece of gold for each one. Po is well known to the English-speaking public, probably more so than most Chinese poets, through Arthur Waley's graceful translation. Po was once appointed Junior Mentor of the heir apparent, a position that was sometimes referred to as "secretary" (*she-jen*).

2. During the T'ang dynasty, Rooster Woods (*Chi-lin*) was a Chinese name for Korea, or, to be more specific, the kingdom of Shilla (Hsin-lo), which unified most of the Korean peninsula in the mid-seventh century. In the year 663 the T'ang emperor issued an order to make Shilla the prefecture of the Rooster Woods and to appoint the king of Shilla as its governor-general.

Yüan Hung-tao

First Trip to West Lake

1. According to Chang Tai's *Searching for West Lake in Dreams*, the Celebration Temple (Chao-ch'ing Ssu) was first built in the tenth century, during the period of the Five Dynasties, in celebration of the eightieth birthday of Ch'ien Liu (852–932), who was enfeoffed by the emperor of the Later Liang as the king of Wu-Yüeh.

2. Prince Tung-o was the title of Ts'ao Ts'ao's son, the poet Ts'ao Chih (192–232), who wrote a rhapsody on the goddess of the River Lo.

3. Tzu-kung was the "style" name of Ho Wen-chuan, who served the author as his personal secretary between 1594 and 1607.

4. Yüeh's Tomb is that of Yüeh Fei (1103–42), the Southern Sung military general who led many victorious battles against the invading Jurchen Chin troops but was later wrongfully maligned and summarily executed.

5. T'ao Wang-ling (1562–1609), a writer and thinker, was a close friend of the author's.

Waiting for the Moon: An Evening Trip to the Six Bridges

1. Chang Kung-fu (Chang Tzu), grandson of the famous Sung general Chang Chün (1086–1154), had his Shining Jade Hall built by West Lake, where he is said to have planted more than three hundred early plum (*Prunus mume*) trees.

2. The Broken Bridge (Tuan Ch'iao) is located at the foot of Solitary Hill by West Lake. It was originally named Pao-yu Bridge, but has been called the Broken Bridge since the T'ang dynasty, as the road that leads from Solitary Hill terminates ("breaks") at the bridge.

A Trip to the Six Bridges after a Rain

1. The Cold Food Day, usually in early April, was a day when people were supposed not to make a fire and therefore had to eat cold food.

Mirror Lake

1. Mirror Lake (Chien Hu) is in southern Shao-hsing Prefecture, Chekiang. It was also known as Director Ho's Pond (Ho-chien Ch'ih).

2. Ho Chih-chang (659–744) was a T'ang poet and a close friend of the great poet Li Po (701–62). Ho once served as director of the Palace Library (*mi-shu-chien*), an appointment in charge of archival and editorial work. For a short period (662–70) during the T'ang, when the Palace Library was called the Orchid Terrace, the director was known as the Grand Scribe (T'ai-shih)—the same title held by the author's friend T'ao Wang-ling, hence the allusion.

3. Li Po, a legendary alcoholic, was sometimes called the Banished Immortal.

A Trip to Brimming Well

1. "Yen" refers to Peking. The southwestern part of the city was the location of the ancient city of Chi, the capital of Yen, one of the feudal states during the Chou dynasty and the period of the Warring States.

2. The Flowers Day Festival is another name for the Birthday of the Flowers. See note 1 to Ch'en Chi-ju's "Trips to See Peach in Bloom."

3. Brimming Well, in the northeastern suburbs of Peking, was a place for sightseeing during the Ming dynasty. There was a fountain spring there, the water of which was said to be frequently overflowing over its brim, hence the name.

4. The author was at this time an educational official at the Confucian school in Shun-t'ien Prefecture.

A Trip to High Beam Bridge

1. During the Ming dynasty, High Beam Bridge spanned the High Beam River, which rose in the Western Hills and flowed east all the way into the imperial palace, where it was called the Jade River.

2. In Ming usage, classmates (*t'ung-nien*) were those who passed the prefectural or metropolitan civil service examination in the same year.

A Biography of the Stupid but Efficient Ones

1. Master of Stone was the author's cognomen.

2. The swallow is known to habitually build its nest under the eaves of houses. As noted in the ancient classic *Erh-ya*, the stork was capable of catching the hunter's arrow and throwing it back. It was observed in the ancient classic *Classic of Birds* (Ch'in-ching) that "the turtledove is stupid but safe." According to the footnote by the Chin writer Chang Hua (232–300), although the turtledove is so stupid it doesn't even know how to build a nest, it just takes over the nest of another bird, notably a magpie's, and stays in perfect ease there.

3. A "capping" ceremony was held for a young man at his twentieth birthday as a symbol of achieving adulthood.

Essay: A Biography of Hsü Wen-ch'ang

This more formal essay is included here along with *hsiao-p'in* by Yüan Hung-tao because of its significance among his works.

1. As commander-in-chief of the troops of several southeastern provinces, Hu Tsung-hsien led many battles against invading Japanese pirates and other insurgents. In 1558 he captured two white deer (considered an auspicious sign) in Chekiang and presented them to Emperor Shih-tsung. Hsü Wei wrote a memorial to the throne for the occasion on his behalf.

2. Liu T'an, a renowned man of letters and a wit, was once a private secretary of Prime Minister Ssu-ma Yü, who later became Emperor Chien-wen of the Eastern Chin (r. 371–72). Tu Fu, the famous T'ang poet, was once a private secretary of Yen Wu, military commissioner of Szechwan.

3. As writers of classical prose, Han Yü and Tseng Kung (1019–83) were ranked among the Eight Prose Masters of the T'ang and Sung.

4. Ou-yang Hsiu, a Northern Sung poet and author, was another of the Eight Prose Masters of the T'ang and Sung.

5. Chang Yüan-pien (1538–88), who won the title of Optimus (*chuang-yüan*, "first place") in the Metropolitan Examination of 1571, was Chang Tai's great-grandfather.

Yüan Chung-tao

Foreword to *The Sea of Misery*

This preface for an anthology of poetry compiled by the author provides a glimpse into the mind of the young Chung-tao, who was only fifteen years old at the time.

1. Yüan Sung was governor of Wu-chün during the Chin dynasty. This refers to an anecdote in *A New Account of Tales of the World* (XXIII, 43).

2. "Transcendence" (*t'an tu*) here refers to the Mahayana Buddhist belief that one should help others in their enlightenment in addition to achieving enlightenment oneself.

3. According to the ancient classic *The Book of Chou Officialdom* (Chou li), which is about the hierarchy, rites, and government structure of the Chou dynasty, the Chime-maker was a low-ranking official in charge of the making of chimes. Here the term refers to the author's social status (as a prefectural school student) at the time.

Shady Terrace

1. The suburbs of Ch'ang-an refers here to the capital, i.e., Peking.

Selections from *Wood Shavings of Daily Life*

Wood Shavings of Daily Life (Yu-chü fei-lu) is the author's diary from 1608 to 1618; the entries in it are mostly undated and probably were not written on a daily basis.

3

1. Matteo Ricci (1552–1610) was a Jesuit missionary from Italy. "Attendant" (*shih-t'sung*) refers vaguely to someone honored with an interview with the emperor.

2. Wang Yang was probably Wang Chi (styled Tzu-yang, d. 48 B.C.E.), a Han dynasty official who was known to live in luxury at home despite a reputation for being free from corruption. Hence he was suspected of possessing the power of alchemy.

4

1. From the twenty-second of the eighth month until the sixth of the ninth month of the year 1610, Yüan Chung-tao's daily diary entries provide a detailed description of how Hung-tao fell sick and died.

5

1. Yü's Tripod is a bronze vessel cast in the late Western Chou period (9th–8th cent. B.C.E.), so called because the inscription on it is a brief account of the military accomplishments of Yü, the founder of the legendary Hsia dynasty. The legendary Mirror of Ch'in, which was said to have the magical power of seeing through one's body and revealing one's mind, was in the possession of the First Emperor of Ch'in.

Chung Hsing

Flower-Washing Brook

1. The Bridge of Ten Thousand Li (Wan-li Ch'iao) in the southern part of the city of Ch'eng-tu, originally the Comet Bridge (Ch'ang-hsing Ch'iao), was renamed after a saying of Chu-ko Liang's. When Fei I was sent on diplomatic errands to the kingdom of Wu, Chu-ko Liang held a farewell party for him at the bridge and remarked, "A travel of ten thousand li is about to start from your first step."

2. When Tu Fu came to Szechwan, he first lived in the western suburbs of Ch'eng-tu, where he named his residence the Flower-Washing Thatched Cottage.

3. The Black Sheep Palace is a T'ang dynasty Taoist temple. The name is based upon a legend about how Lao-tzu, canonized as the founder of Taoism, once visited this place on the back of a black sheep.

4. From one of Tu Fu's poems. Kuan-hsien County was also known as Kuan-k'ou (lit., "mouth of the Kuan River") in earlier times.

5. Commandant Chu-ko Liang's Shrine still stands in the suburbs of Ch'eng-tu today.

6. Tu Fu was once appointed vice-director of the Ministry of Works and traditionally was often referred to by his official title. Vice-Director Tu's Shrine, located at the site of the Flower-Washing Thatched Cottage rebuilt during the Sung dynasty, is still a favorite tourist attraction.

7. Tu Fu has often been referred to as Tu the Senior so as to distinguish him from Tu Mu (803–52?), a later poet who was called Tu the Junior, though unrelated to the former.

8. After Yen Wu's death, Tu Fu moved from Ch'eng-tu to K'uei-chou (K'uei-meng) along the Yangtze and lived in a place called the Eastern Garrison, so named because it was the site where Kung-sun Shu (d. C.E. 36), a warlord of the Eastern Han, led his garrison troops to open up wasteland east of K'uei-chou for agriculture.

9. This is from the biography of Confucius in Ssu-ma Ch'ien's *Historical Records*.

10. Ching-ling, the author's native town, was a part of the ancient kingdom of Ch'u.

To Ch'en Chi-ju

Ch'en Chi-ju was sixteen years older than Chung.

A Colophon to My Poetry Collection

1. "Notable" (*ming shih*) originally referred to one who had become famous but had no official appointment. In the late Ming context the term became fashionable and was principally used for literati who chose not to adhere to social norms. The author was obviously contemptuous of those who claimed to be such notables.

A Colophon to *A Drinker's Manual*

1. One of Ts'ao Ts'ao's poems starts with the carpe diem lines "In front of wine, one is to sing! / How brief human life is."

2. Hsieh An (320–85) was a statesman of the Eastern Chin. In 383, when he served as prime minister during Emperor Hsiao-wu-ti's reign (373–96), the Eastern Chin troops, numbering some eighty thousand men, defeated the invading army (who claimed to be nine hundred thousand strong) of the northern regime of the Former Ch'in in the famous Battle of Fei-shui. This anecdote about Hsieh An is found in *A New Account of Tales of the World* (VI, 35).

3. One *tan* equals approximately 26 gallons. Notice the literary hyperbole here.

4. Li Po, who wrote many poems about drinking, was known as one of the Eight Immortals among Drinkers.

5. *The Analects* (X, 8).

6. From Ssu-ma Ch'ien's *Historical Records* ("The Biographies of the Humorists"). This was Ch'un-yü K'un's response to a question from King Wei-wang about his capacity for drinking. Ch'un-yü was an erudite scholar who served under the king of the Ch'i during the period of the Warring States. A *tou* equals approximately 2.6 gallons; 10 *tou* equal one *tan*.

Inscription on My Portrait

1. P'ei Tu (765–839) was a T'ang dynasty statesman.

Li Liu-fang

A Short Note about My Trips to Tiger Hill

1. The Mid-Autumn Festival falls on the fifteenth day of the eighth month in the Chinese lunar calendar. The full moon on that night is equivalent to the English "harvest moon" (the full moon nearest the autumnal equinox).

2. This line alludes to a famous remark by Confucius in *The Analects* (IX, 27): "Only in the depth of winter do we realize that the pine and the cypress are the last to shed their leaves."

A Short Note about My Trips to Boulder Lake

1. Boulder Lake (Shih Hu) is southwest of Soochow. To its north is Horizontal Pond, to its southwest is Lake T'ai-hu, and to its east is the Grand Canal at the Hsü Gate of Soochow City. The Sung poet Fan Ch'eng-ta (1126–93), who lived there in retirement, adopted the cognomen Lay Buddhist at Boulder Lake.

2. Meng-yang was the "style" name of Ch'eng Chia-sui (1565–1644). As poets and landscape painters, Ch'eng and the author, along with T'ang Shih-sheng (1551–1636) and Lou Chien (1567–1631), were known as the Four Masters of Chiating. Ch'eng was also one of the Nine Painter Friends.

3. "Height-ascending," usually a drinking party atop a hill, is a custom observed on the Double Ninth Festival (the ninth day of the ninth month of the lunar calendar). It originated from a story in a collection of supernatural tales by Wu Chün (469–520) of the Liang dynasty. Fei Chang-fang, a Taoist of the Eastern Han period, once told his disciple Huan Ching that his family was to suffer a disaster on the ninth day of the ninth month. To avoid the disaster, everyone in the family had to tie a bagful of ailanthus prickly ash (*Zanthoxylum ailanthoides*) flowers and leaves around the arm, ascend to a high place, and drink some wine brewed with chrysanthemum flowers. Huan did as he was instructed and took his family atop a hill. When they went home at dusk they found that all the fowl, dogs, cattle, and sheep left there were dead.

Inscriptions on *An Album of Recumbent Travels in Chiang-nan*

Horizontal Pond
1. Hsü Gate, named in memory of Wu Tzu-hsü (d. 484 B.C.E.), the military commander of the ancient kingdom of Wu, is in the western city wall of Soochow, formerly the capital of Wu. The Ch'ang Gate is also along the western city wall.
2. Wu-lin, also known as Ling-yin Hill, is in the western suburbs of Hangchow. The term is often used to refer to Hangchow in general.

Boulder Lake
1. "Cap-dropping party" refers to an anecdote in *A New Account of Tales of the World* (VII, 16). The handsome Meng Chia, who was the maternal grandfather of the poet T'ao Yüan-ming, once attended a "height-ascending" party with his colleagues. All in the company except Meng were dressed in formal military attire, but he was admired by everyone for his graceful carriage when he sat and drank at ease, unaware that the wind had blown his cap off.

Tiger Hill
1. This alludes to a story from the ancient classic *Lü's Spring and Autumn Annals* (Lü-shih ch'un-ch'iu), compiled by retainers of Lü Pu-wei (d. 235 B.C.E.), the prime minister of the kingdom of Ch'in. Deserted by all his family and relatives because of his strong body odor, a man lived in seclusion by the sea. There he met a man who was addicted to the stench of his body odor and followed him around all day and night.

Divinity Cliff
1. On Hsi Shih, see p. 117, note 2 to Ch'en Chi-ju's "A Colophon to *A Profile of Yao P'ing-chung*." King Fu-ch'ai built for her a palace known as the Belle's Lodge (Kuan-wa Kung) at Divinity Cliff in the western suburbs of Soochow.

Inscription on *A Picture of Solitary Hill on a Moonlit Night*

1. The West Fall (Hsi-ling) is a bridge by West Lake. It is at the foot of Solitary Hill (Ku-shan).

Wang Ssu-jen

A Trip to Brimming Well

Compare this piece with Yüan Hung-tao's travel note on Brimming Well in this collection.

A Trip to Wisdom Hill and Tin Hill

1. Wisdom Hill and Tin Hill are in the western suburbs of Wu-hsi, Kiangsu. Water from Wisdom Hill fountain has been known as the "second best in the world" for tea making, and clay statuettes are a famous local product. The ancient kingdom of Yüeh covered a large part of modern Chekiang. In 473 B.C.E., led by King Kou-chien, the Yüeh troops eliminated the kingdom of Wu and expanded their territory into Kiangsu. The author was a native of Shan-yin, Chekiang, so he often claimed to be a "native of Yüeh."

2. Ssu-ma Hsiang-ju (179–117 B.C.E.), the famous Han dynasty rhapsody writer, met the beautiful widowed Cho Wen-chün at her father's house. They fell in love at first sight and eloped. After marriage they ran a tavern, with Wen-chün herself serving their customers.

3. *Ting-yüan*, as a title for Sun, could refer to either *ting-chia* (one of the top three men among those who passed a Palace Examination, the culmination of the triennial civil-service recruitment examination sequence), or *ting-k'uei* (the Metropolitan Graduate whose name stood in third place on that list). *Hui-pang*, used as a title for Hua, could be a variation of Principal Graduate (Hui-yüan), the man ranked first in the Metropolitan Examination. Both the Suns and the Huas were prominent families of Wu-hsi. These two men were probably local celebrities.

4. According to traditional Chinese geomancy (*feng-shui*), terrestrial veins at the location of a house or tomb guarantee the prosperity of the family.

5. Yeh Fa-shan was a Taoist priest who served several T'ang emperors, including Emperor Hsüan-tsung. He is said to have had some magic power, and to have brought the spirit of Yang Yü-huan, the imperial consort, for a reunion with the emperor. Hsüan-tsung (685–762, r. 712–56) was the third son of Emperor Jui-tsung, hence in folk literature he was often referred to as the Third Brother. His tragic love affair with Yang Yü-huan was immortalized in Po Chü-i's famous poem *Song of Everlasting Sorrow*. Kuang-ling was an old name for the city of Yangchow.

Passing by the Small Ocean

1. Mount Kua-ts'ang is in southeast Chekiang. The Evil Brook (O-hsi), later known as the Good Brook, flows through several southwestern counties in Chekiang. It was so named because it was once said to have been haunted by evil spirits.

2. The Small Ocean (Hsiao-yang), so named because of its relative broadness, is a tributary in the lower reaches of the Evil Brook.

3. The yellow-helmeted gentlemen (*huang-t'ou lang*) were members of the palace

guard in charge of imperial navigation during the Han dynasty. The term is used here for the boatmen.

4. Siddhartha was the name of Buddha (ca. 563–ca. 483 B.C.E.).

5. The author alludes to Tu Fu's lines from his poem "Looking at Mt. T'ai-shan in the Distance": "My agitated bosom gives rise to layers of clouds / My straining eyes chase the home-going birds."

6. Chinese traditionally believed that there were five primary colors: green, red, yellow, white, and black.

Shan-hsi Brook

1. Ts'ao O was a girl of the Han dynasty known for her filial piety. When her father was drowned, fourteen-year-old Ts'ao O walked along the river in tears, trying to find his corpse. When she failed, she drowned herself. The Ts'ao O River flows through Shao-hsing County in eastern Chekiang; Shan-hsi Brook is part of its upper reaches.

2. Located in what is now the town of Riverside (Ling-chiang Chen), the Junction of Three Counties was where Shang-yü, Shao-hsing, and Sheng-hsien joined.

3. The Cool Breeze Ridge (Ch'ing-feng Ling) is north of the town of Sheng-hsien. In 1276 Lady Wang of Lin-hai County was carried off by Mongol troops. The next year, when the troops passed by the Cool Breeze Ridge, she bit her finger and used her own blood to write a poem on the cliff, and then killed herself by jumping off the precipice. Later a shrine was built there in her honor.

4. Green leaves and red flowers.

5. Wang Hsien-chih, son of the famous "sage of calligraphy" Wang Hsi-chih, was also a great calligrapher known as Wang the Junior. Here the author quotes a line from his description of the beautiful views in Shan-yin County, Chekiang: "Throughout Shan-yin County, the mountains and the rivers set off and outshine one another, overwhelming viewers. Between autumn and winter it would be even more exhilarating" (*A New Account of Tales of the World* [II, 91]).

6. Wang Hui-chih (styled Tzu-yu, d. 388) was also a son of Wang Hsi-chih's. One night when he lived in Shan-yin, he woke up during a heavy snow and had a drink. Then he suddenly missed his friend, the famous scholar, sculptor, and painter Tai K'uei (d. 396), who lived along Shan-hsi Brook. Wang immediately went there in a small boat. The trip took all night. When he arrived at Tai's gate at dawn, he suddenly changed his mind and went back. On being asked why, he replied, "I went at the peak of my enthusiasm, and turned back when my enthusiasm was gone. Why must I see Tai?" The anecdote is found in *A New Account of Tales of the World* (XXIII, 47). The author was not known to be a direct descendant of the calligrapher's family; he jokingly refers to Wang Hui-chih as "Tzu-yu of our family" because they shared the family name Wang.

7. One *chang* equals approximately 11 feet 8 inches.

8. According to a Chinese myth, the rainbow stoops down from heaven to drink from the earth.

9. Sun Ch'u (218–93) was a man of letters of the Western Chin dynasty. When he was young, Sun once wanted to tell a friend about his desire to become a recluse,

about how he would like to "pillow his head upon the pebbles and brush his teeth in the stream." But he stumbled and said instead that he would like to "pillow his head on the stream and brush his teeth upon the pebbles." His stunned friend asked, "You may be able to use the stream as pillow, but how can you brush your teeth upon the pebbles?" The quick-witted Sun replied, "I want to use the stream as my pillow so that I can wash my ears in it, and I want to brush my teeth upon the pebbles so that I can have them sharpened." In Chinese the phrase "sharp teeth" is tantamount to the English phrase "sharp tongue." This anecdote is from *A New Account of Tales of the World* (XXV, 6).

T'an Yüan-ch'un

First Trip to Black Dragon Pond

Black Dragon Pond (Wu-lung T'an), located at the foot of Cooler Hill in the western part of Nanking, is so named because a black dragon was said to have emerged from the pond during the Chin dynasty.

1. During the period of the Six Dynasties (222–80, 317–589) Chien-k'ang (later known as Nanking) was the capital of several regimes in south China. The southern gate of the city was also called the White Gate, so Nanking was often referred to as the White Gate, especially in poetic and literary usage.

2. The Swallow Rock (Yen-tzu Chi), a famous resort, is located on the bank of the Yangtze in the northeastern suburbs of Nanking.

3. Mo-ch'ou Lake, named after the legendary singing girl Mo-ch'ou (lit., "No Sorrow"), is located right outside the Waterway West Gate of Nanking.

4. According to Taoist belief, the Black Turtle (Hsüan-wu)—in the image of a turtle, or in another version, the duality of a turtle and a snake—is one of the deities representing the four directions: Black Turtle for the north, Red Bird the south, Green Dragon the east, and White Tiger the west. Black Turtle Lake is outside the Black Turtle Gate along the northeastern city wall of Nanking.

5. On the Ch'in-huai River, see p. 114, note 2 to T'u Lung's "A Letter in Reply to Li Wei-yin."

6. Mao Yüan-i (styled Chih-sheng) was the grandson of the famous essayist Mao K'un.

Second Trip to Black Dragon Pond

1. The Seventh Evening is that of the seventh month in the Chinese lunar calendar. It was to be the night when the Cowherd (the star Altair) and the Weaver Maid (the star Vega) made their annual rendezvous by the Heavenly River, or River of Stars (the Milky Way).

2. This refers to the canopy of the raft. Mao Yüan-i built his raft in the shape of a canopied tent. See "First Trip to Black Dragon Pond."

3. Wu Ting-fang (styled Ning-fu) was a poet who later became a Buddhist monk. Both Mao Yü-ch'ang (styled Po-ling) and Hung K'uan (styled Chung-wei) were poets.

Third Trip to Black Dragon Pond

1. The two gates along the western city wall of Nanking were the Waterway West Gate and the Overland West Gate. The latter was also called Cooler Gate because it was close to Cooler Hill.

2. The Hua-lin Garden, site of the royal palace of the kingdom of Wu during the period of the Three Kingdoms, was frequented by nobility during the Southern Dynasties. Lord Hsieh's Mound, at the foot of Mount Chung-shan, was a garden built in the Chin dynasty by Hsieh An. During the Sung dynasty it was once renamed Mid-Hill Garden by its new owner, the statesman and writer Wang An-shih (1021–86), who lived there in retirement after dismissal from the position of prime minister.

3. Cooler Hill, also known as Stone Hill, is located in the western part of Nanking. Nanking is sometimes called the Stone City because of the hill.

Chang Tai

Selections from *Dream Memories from the T'ao Hut*

A Night Performance at Golden Hill

1. Golden Hill (Chin-shan) is northwest of Chen-chiang City. The Golden Hill Temple, built in the Eastern Chin dynasty, is one of the oldest Buddhist temples in China.

2. See Ch'en Chi-ju's *Privacies in the Mountains*, selection 1, note 1 (this volume). The second beat was two hours before midnight (the third beat).

3. Han Shih-chung (1089–1151) was a military general who led the Southern Sung troops in a victorious battle against the invading Jurchen Chin army at the foot of Golden Hill.

Plum Blossoms Bookroom

1. During the Eastern Chin dynasty, a military garrison was set up at Yü-chou, west of the capital, Chien-k'ang (Nanking). It was called the West Garrison (Hsi Fu). The West Garrison crab apple is a dwarf tree with red flowers, originally from Yü-chou, hence the name.

2. Lake T'ai-hu rock is a porous rock used in garden rockeries.

3. The West Brook (Hsi Hsi) is one of the Nine Brooks and Eighteen Gullies, a chief tourist attraction northwest of Ling-yin Hill in Hangchow.

4. The Obtuse Ni (Ni Yü) was the nickname for Ni Tsan (1301–74), a great landscape painter of the Yüan dynasty. He built a house for his private collection of books and paintings, which he named Pavilion of Quiet Privacy (Ch'ing-pi Ko). Like the author, Ni was born and brought up in a rich family, but, due to the social upheavals with the change of regime (from the Yüan to the Ming), he had to give up his property and lead a recluse's life. His cognomen was Cloud Forest (Yün-lin).

Drinking Tea at Pop Min's

1. Min Hsien (styled Wen-shui) was a potter from Shantung famous for making I-hsing style porcelain tea sets.

2. After Emperor Ch'eng-tsu moved the capital to Peking, Nanking was designated the "reserved capital" (*liu tu*).

3. The Ching-hsi Brook flows through I-hsing County, Kiangsu, which is famous for its tea vessels.

4. Emperor Hsüan-tsung's Hsüan-te reign (1426–35) and Emperor Hsien-tsung's Ch'eng-hua reign (1465–87) were famous for their fine porcelain products.

5. Lo-chieh tea is produced in Ch'ang-hsing County, Chekiang.

6. Favor Hill is also known as Wisdom Hill. See Wang Ssu-jen's "A Trip to Wisdom Hill and Tin Hill" (this volume).

7. Tea fanciers prefer the new crop (*hsin ch'a*), which is picked in the spring.

Viewing the Snow from the Mid-Lake Gazebo

1. The last beat of the night watch is just before dawn.

2. Chin-ling was an old name for Nanking.

Yao Chien-shu's Paintings

1. Yao Yün-tsai (styled Chien-shu) was a late Ming painter from Chekiang.

2. The painter brothers Wei Chih-huang and Wei Chih-k'o were natives of Nanking.

3. Tseng Ching (styled Po-ch'en, 1564–1647) was a painter from Fukien.

4. Su Han-ch'en was a painter at the Imperial Academy during the Sung dynasty.

Moon at Censer Peak

1. Censer Peak is one of the famous peaks of Mount Lu-shan, located by the Yangtze in northern Kiangsi.

2. This height is obviously rhetorical.

3. Wang Shou-jen (posthumously designated Lord Wen-ch'eng) was a Ming philosopher and statesman better known by his cognomen Master Yang-ming. He once served as governor of Kiangsi.

4. Hsieh Ling-yün (385–433) is generally considered to be the father of Chinese landscape poetry. He was fond of traveling in the mountains of Chekiang and once opened a road through the mountains from Shih-ning to Lin-hai (where Wang Hsiu served as governor). See J. D. Frodsham, *The Murmuring Stream: The Life and Works of the Chinese Nature Poet Hsieh Ling-yün (385–433), Duke of K'ang-lo* (Kuala Lumpur: University of Malaya Press, 1967).

Liu Ching-t'ing the Storyteller

1. Pockmarked Liu (Liu Ma-tzu) was the sobriquet people gave to Liu Ching-t'ing, who was originally named Ts'ao Yü-ch'un but changed his name in youth when he ran away from home as a fugitive after getting in trouble with the local government. Liu became extremely popular as a professional storyteller in Nanking. As a celebrity, he had connections among dignitaries and, after the downfall of the Ming, served in the Southern Ming regime as an assistant to General Tso Liang-yü (1599–1645). Like Chang Tai, Liu lived into his eighties and died in oblivion and poverty. He was fictionalized as a major figure in the famous historical drama *The Peach Blossom Fan* by K'ung Shang-jen (1648–1718).

2. This description of Liu Ling, one of the Seven Sages in the Bamboo Grove of the Chin dynasty and a legendary alcoholic, is from *A New Account of Tales of the World* (XIV, "Looks and Manners," 13).

3. Wang Yüeh-sheng was a renowned courtesan in Nanking. See Chang Tai's sketch of her in this anthology.

4. "Wu Sung Knocks Out the Tiger at Ching-yang Ridge" is an episode from the famous Chinese novel *Water Margin*.

West Lake on the Fifteenth Night of the Seventh Month

1. The fifteenth night of the seventh lunar month (lit., "mid-seventh month") was a Taoist festival called the Mid-Year Festival (Chung-yüan Chieh).

2. Gatekeepers were tipped for keeping the city gates open later than usual.

Wang Yüeh-sheng

1. The Vermilion Market and Crooked Lane were late Ming red-light districts in Nanking.

Crab Parties

1. The five flavors are sweet, sour, bitter, hot, and salty. "Five flavors" refers to flavors in general.

2. The quantity and richness of the roe of the female and the milt of the male freshwater crabs from the lakes and ponds around Soochow grant them their special status as great delicacies.

3. The "eight treasures" are delicacies, mostly game food. The list, varying through the ages, includes such rarities as bear's paw, orangutan's lips, and camel's hump.

4. Jade-Pot Ice is a kind of liquor. Yüan Tsung-tao wrote a rhapsody in celebration of it.

5. In another piece in *Dream Memories*, the author tells how he personally made the experiments that led to the production of a new kind of tea, which he named Snow Orchid. In a few years it became extremely popular with the public.

Lang-hsüan, Land of Enchantment

This is the last piece in *Dream Memories from the T'ao Hut*. The title originates from a collection of short sketches and stories, *Notes of Lang-hsüan*, attributed to I Shih-chen of the Yüan dynasty. The first entry tells how Chang Hua (232–300), poet and statesman of the Chin dynasty, once came into a grotto and found a magnificent palace inside, where every room was filled with strange books about pre-Han historical events. He was told that the place was called Lang-hsüan, Land of Enchantment (Lang-hsüan Fu-ti). Chang Tai was obviously fascinated by the story, as he also titled the collection of his poetry and more formal essays *Collection of Literary Works from Lang-hsüan*.

1. The ancient inscription script (*chuan shu*) was used mainly on seals.

2. The *so-lo* is a big evergreen dragonhead tree that belongs to the genus *Dracocephalum*. It has terminal spikes of rose-pink or purplish flowers that bloom in midsummer. It was under such a tree that Buddha is said to have passed away and attained nirvana.

3. In traditional usage, "one hill and one dale" (*i ch'iu i ho*) refers to a recluse's retreat.

4. Both Taoists and Buddhists compare death to the sloughing of a cicada, hence the decease of a believer is often referred to as "exuviation."

5. "Chang-kung" (Eldest Son) was used as the author's "style" name in the epitaph he wrote for himself, following the tradition of one who was the eldest son in his family.

6. Mount Ching-t'ing (lit., "Homage Gazebo") is located in southern Anhwei, across the Yangtze from Censer Peak in Mount Lu-shan. The gazebo on it was said to have been the site where Hsieh T'iao (464–99), a poet of the Southern Dynasties (Ch'i), composed his poems. The mountain has also become famous from a quatrain, "Sitting Alone in Front of Mt. Chingt'ing," by the great T'ang poet Li Po.

An Epitaph for Myself

The great poet T'ao Ch'ien, whom Chang Tai admired (the author's cognomen, T'ao Hut, was in his honor), wrote "A Funeral Speech for Myself" and initiated this subgenre of literary prose.

1. The Pear Garden was located inside the Forbidden Palace in Ch'ang-an. At the imperial order of T'ang emperor Hsüan-tsung, three hundred musicians and several hundred palace maids were housed there to study singing and dancing. The term "Pear Garden" referred to theater in general.

2. The following passage is modeled on the famous "Letter to Shan T'ao" by Hsi K'ang (223–62), one of the Seven Sages of the Bamboo Grove, who named seven things he could not stand in society. For an English translation of the letter by J. R. Hightower, see Birch, comp. and ed., *Anthology of Chinese Literature: From Early Times to the Fourteenth Century*, pp. 162–66.

3. Golden Valley was the family garden owned by Shih Ch'ung (242–300), a high-ranking official of the Chin dynasty known for his wealth and extravagant lifestyle.

4. This is from a story in the ancient classic *Han-fei-tzu*. A hare ran into the stump of a tree and dropped dead. A farmer saw and picked it up. He gave up farming and waited by the stump, hoping for another windfall.

5. During the period of the Warring States, Ch'en Chung-tzu, a native of Ch'u, left his home because of disagreement with his elder brother on a matter of principle. He settled down at Yü-ling in the state of Ch'u and became known as the Master of Yü-ling. The king of Ch'u wanted to appoint him prime minister because of his reputation, but he ran away again and lived the rest of his life as a gardener. In literature Yü-ling often signifies a retreat or hermitage.

6. In the Taoist tradition the Jade Emperor (Yü-huang Ta-ti) is the supreme deity, who governs in the Celestial Palace.

7. A citation from a story in the biography of Lou Shih-te (630–99), who in 693 was promoted to the position of grand councilor, in *New History of the T'ang* (Hsin T'ang-shu). Once Lou and his younger brother discussed the art of exercising restraint. His brother said, "If someone spits on me, I'll just clean it up." Lou said,

"That's not enough. If you wipe it clean, you'll stir up more anger. You should just let it dry off by itself."

8. Under the traditional patriarchal system, "Tsung-tzu" meant the eldest son of the wife, as distinguished from the son of a concubine. Chang Tai's other "style" name and his cognomen were similar to those used by preceding Ming authors whom he admired: Shih-kung (Master of Stone) had been adopted by Yüan Hung-tao, and T'ao-an (Tao Hut) by Kuei Yu-kuang.

9. Of the fifteen works listed here, seven have been lost (nos. 2, 5, 6, 10, 11, 13, and 15). The fifth and sixth works are obviously studies of the *I Ching*, an ancient manual for fortune-tellers and one of the six Confucian classics. The title of no. 13 is based upon an anecdote about the T'ang poet Li Ho (790–816) as recounted in *A Short Biography of Li Ch'ang-chi* by the late-T'ang poet Li Shang-yin (813–58). When Li Ho rode out on the back of a donkey, he always had a servant boy carrying an old embroidered bag follow him on foot. Whenever Li Ho felt inspired and thought of some lines, he would write them down on a slip of paper and throw it into the bag.

10. Chang Tai's father, Chang Yao-fang (cognomen Ta-t'i), served as administrator under the prince of Lu. The position, chief executive official in a princely establishment (*wang-fu*), was also known as *kuo-hsiang*, counselor-delegate. During the Ming, Lady of Suitability (I-jen) was the honorific title granted to wives of fifth-tier officials.

11. Note that the author switches here to the use of the first-person singular pronoun to refer to himself.

12. Chang Tai's grandfather Chang Ju-lin (cognomen, Yü-jo), a Metropolitan Graduate of 1595, once served as a secretary (*chu-shih*) in the Ministry of War.

13. Master Mei-kung was the cognomen of Ch'en Chi-ju. "To strike at the autumn wind" is a vernacular phrase that means "to call on someone for money or gifts through social connections."

14. Wang Chi (d. 644) was an early T'ang poet. Following the example of T'ao Yüan-ming, both Wang Chi and Hsü Wei wrote epitaphs for themselves.

15. "Knit my brows in imitation," referring to blind imitation with ludicrous effect, is derived from a story in *Chuang-tzu* (chap. "The Heavenly Way"). An ugly woman named Tung (East) Shih knitted her brows in imitation of her neighbor Hsi (West) Shih, the celebrated beauty of the state of Yüeh, only to make herself look uglier.

16. Hsiang-wang was Hsiang Yü (232–202 B.C.E.), an aristocrat of the Ch'u kingdom and rebel leader who fought against and overthrew the Ch'in empire. He was defeated in battle by his rival Liu Pang (who later became the first emperor of the Han dynasty) and killed himself. By identifying himself with a rebel, the author showed his indignation against the Manchu regime.

17. Liang Hung was a first-century recluse who lived in the mountains (probably on Mount Chickenhead) with his loving wife, Meng Kuang. Yao Li was a swordsman of the Wu kingdom of fifth century B.C.E. who successfully carried out a suicidal mission to assassinate Prince Ch'ing-chi, the king's political rival.

18. This is from a story in *Han-fei-tzu*. Pien Ho, a Ch'u native, found a piece of uncut precious jade at Mount Ching and presented it to King Li-wang, who thought it was a fake and had Pien's left foot cut off. When King Li-wang died, Pien again

presented the jade to the new king, Wu-wang; this time he got his right foot cut off. When the next king, Wen-wang, succeeded to the throne, he was told that Pien was crying at Mount Ching, holding the uncut jade in his arms. The king ordered a jade artisan to work on it and found it really to be a precious jade. It was later known as Ho's Jade.

19. Lien P'o was a famous general of the kingdom of Chao. In 251 B.C.E., after winning a war, Lien was made counselor-in-chief, but he was disfavored by the next king and later died in exile. Cho-lu, now in Hopei Province, is known as the site of an ancient battlefield where the legendary Yellow Emperor (Huang-ti) defeated Ch'ih-yu.

20. This refers to the great Han historian Ssu-ma Ch'ien. Dragon Gate (*Lung-meng*), the name of a county in Honan, was his birthplace. One interpretation of the term "sham" (*yen*) used here is that it refers to Ssu-ma Ch'ien's castration, after which he was no longer considered to be a "real" man. Since in the entire epilogue the author compares himself to these historical figures, it may be an expression of modesty, implying that the author himself was not a "real" historian like Ssu-ma Ch'ien.

21. Eastern Slope (Tung-p'o) was the cognomen of the great Sung writer Su Shih, also known as a gourmet. Some Chinese dishes, including Tung-p'o Pork, are said to have been invented by him while he lived in exile on Hai-nan Island.

22. Solitary Bamboo (Ku-chu) was an ancient state known as the home of Po I and Shu Ch'i, the two sons of the Lord of Ku-chu, who refused to inherit their father's rank and went in exile to the state of Chou. When King Wu-wang of Chou conquered the kingdom of Shang and founded the Chou dynasty, they went into the mountains and died of hunger there. They were acclaimed by Confucius in *The Analects* as men of high principles.

23. Duke Mu-kung of the state of Ch'in (r. 659–21 B.C.E.) ransomed Pai-li Hsi from the state of Ch'u, where the latter was held as a slave, for the price of five black ram skins. Known as the Grand Master (Ta Fu) of Five Black Rams, Pai-li Hsi helped Duke Mu-kung to become a leader of the feudal lords, known as one of the Five Hegemonies (Wu Pa).

24. Mei Fu was an official of the Han in the early first century B.C.E. When Wang Mang (45 B.C.E.–C.E. 23) usurped the throne and founded the short-lived Hsin dynasty, Mei Fu left his family and went into exile. Several years later he was found to be working as a gatekeeper in a southern city under an assumed name. He was said to have subsequently become an Taoist Immortal.

Preface to *Searching for West Lake in Dreams*

1. Shang Chou-tso was minister of personnel in Nanking. Ch'i Piao-chia, a famous prose writer and a relative by marriage of the author, was assistant censor-in-chief and grand coordinator in Chiang-nan. Ch'ien Hsiang-k'un was grand secretary of the Eastern Hall. Yü Huang was senior compiler at the Han-lin Academy. All of these courtiers owned residences by West Lake.

2. Li Po, who served as court attendant under T'ang emperor Hsüan-tsung, wrote a famous poem about a dream trip to Mount T'ien-mu in Chekiang.

3. Here the author alludes to a famous passage from *Chuang-tzu* (chap. "The Equality of Things"): "Once upon a time, Chuang Chou dreamed that he was a butterfly that flitted around happily, enjoying himself without knowing that he was Chou. Suddenly he woke up, and in a startle realized that he *was* Chou."

4. Golden Mincemeat is a famous Chiang-nan–style dish made of fish cooked with peeled and finely cut tangerine slices. Jade Columns is a dish of cooked scallops.

5. Chien-chou (Sword County), where Chang Tai's ancestors once lived, was located at what is now the town of Chien-ko, Szechwan.

Bibliography

Primary Texts

Translator's note: Whenever possible, I have used the most recent scholarly editions of the works of these authors. In the following list each piece is traced to its original section (*chüan*) number (if available) and its page number(s) in the specified edition.

Chang Tai

Chang Tai shih wen chi (Poetry and prose of Chang Tai). Edited by Hsia Hsien-ch'un. Shanghai: Shanghai ku-chi ch'u-pan-she, 1991. "An Epitaph for Myself" (294–97).

Hsi-hu meng-hsün (Searching for West Lake in dreams). Edited and annotated by Sun Chia-sui. Hangchow: Chekiang wen-i ch'u-pan-she, 1985. "Preface to *Searching for West Lake in Dreams*" (1–2).

T'ao-an meng-i (Dream memories from the T'ao Hut). Edited by Chang Hsiao-t'ien. *Ts'ung-shu chi-ch'eng* edition. Ch'ang-sha: Shang-wu yin-shu-kuan, 1939. "A Night Performance at Golden Hill" (1.4); "Plum Blossoms Bookroom" (2.14); "Drinking Tea at Pop Min's" (3.20–21); "Viewing the Snow from the Mid-Lake Gazebo" (3.24); "Yao Chien-shu's Paintings" (5.38–39); "Moon at Censer Peak" (5.39); "Liu Ching-t'ing the Storyteller" (5.40–41); "West Lake on the Fifteenth Night of the Seventh Month" (7.58–59); "Wang Yüeh-sheng" (8.68); "Crab Parties" (8.71); "Lang-hsüan, Land of Enchantment" (8.74).

Ch'en Chi-ju

Ch'en Mei-kung ch'üan-chi (Complete works of Ch'en Mei-kung). 2 vols. Shanghai: Chung-yang shu-tien, 1936. "A Colophon to *A Profile of Yao P'ing-chung*" (II. 210–11).

Wan-hsiang-t'ang chi (Works from the Evening Fragrance Hall). Tsui-lü chü, ed. Ca. 1636. 10 *chüan*. "Trips to See Peach in Bloom" (5.3a–4b); "Inscription on Wang Chung-tsun's *A History of Flowers*" (10.2a–2b); "A Colophon to *A History of Flowers*" (10.8a).

Yen-ch'i yu-shih (Privacies in the mountains). Shanghai: Shang-wu yin-shu-kuan, 1936. "Selections from *Privacies in the Mountains*" (3, 4, 5, 9, 10, 11).

136

Chung Hsing

Yin-hsiu-hsüan chi (Works from the Belvedere of Latent Salience). Edited by Li Hsien-keng and Ts'ui Ch'ung-ch'ing. Shanghai: Shanghai ku-chi ch'u-pan-she, 1992. "Flower-Washing Brook" (20.328–29); "To Ch'en Chi-ju" (28.475–76); "A Colophon to My Poetry Collection" (35.560–61); "Colophon to *A Drinker's Manual* (Four Passages)" (35.567–68); "Inscription after Yüan Hung-tao's Calligraphy" (35.578); "Inscription on My Portrait" (35.583).

Hsü Wei

Hsü Wei chi (Works of Hsü Wei). 4 vols. Peking: Chung-hua shu-chü, 1983.

Hsü Wen-ch'ang san chi (The Third Collection of Hsü Wen-ch'ang's Works): "To Ma Ts'e-chih" (16.II:83); "Foreword to Yeh Tzu-shu's Poetry" (18.II:519–20); "Another Colophon (On the Modern Script 'The Seventeenth' in the Collection of Minister Chu of the Imperial Stud)" (20.II:575).

Hsü Wen-ch'ang yi-kao (Posthumous Works of Hsü Wen-ch'ang): "A Dream" (24.III:1055–56).

Kuei Yu-kuang

Cheng-ch'uan hsien-sheng chi (Works of Master Cheng-ch'uan). Edited by Chou Pen-ch'un. 2 vols. Shanghai: Shanghai ku-chi ch'u-pan-she, 1981. "Foreword to 'Reflections on *The Book of Documents*'" (2.I:50–51); "A Parable of Urns" (4.I:101); "Inscription on the Wall of the Wild Crane Belvedere" (15.I: 399–400); "The Craggy Gazebo" (17.I:427); "The Hsiang-chi Belvedere" (17.I:429–431); "An Epitaph for Chillyposy" (22.II:536).

Li Chih

Fen shu (A book to be burned) and *Hsü Fen shu* (A second book to be burned). Peking: Chung-hua shu-chü, 1975.

Fen shu: "Three Fools" (3.106–7); "In Praise of Liu Hsieh" (3.130); "A Lament for the Passing" (4.164); "On the Mind of a Child" (3.98–99).

Hsü Fen shu: "Inscription on a Portrait of Confucius at the Iris Buddhist Shrine" (4.100).

Li Liu-fang

Mei-shu ts'ung-shu ch'u-chi (A library of fine arts: First series). Edited by Huang Ping-hung and Teng Shih. No. 10. 4th ed. Shanghai: Shen-chou kuo-kuang she, 1947. "Inscription on *A Picture of Solitary Hill on a Moonlit Night*" (142–43).

Wan-Ming erh-shih-chia hsiao-p'in (Vignettes of twenty late Ming authors). "A Short Note about My Trips to Tiger Hill" (185); "A Short Note about My Trips to Boulder Lake" (185–86); "Inscriptions on *An Album of Recumbent Travels in Chiang-nan* (Four Passages)" (189–91).

Lu Shu-sheng

Wan-Ming erh-shih-chia hsiao-p'in. Edited by Shih Che-ts'un. Shanghai: Kuang-ming shu-chü, 1935. "Inkslab Den" (18–19); "Bitter Bamboo" (19); "A Trip to

Wei Village" (21–22); "A Short Note about My Six Attendants in Retirement" (22); "Inscription on Two Paintings in My Collection" (23); "Inscription on a Portrait of Tung-p'o Wearing Bamboo Hat and Clogs" (24).

T'an Yüan-ch'un

T'an Yu-hsia ho-chi (Collected writings of T'an Yu-hsia). Edited by Kung Fu-ch'u. Shanghai: Shen-chou kuo-kuang she, 1935. "First Trip to Black Dragon Pond" (11.145); "Second Trip to Black Dragon Pond" (11.146); "Third Trip to Black Dragon Pond" (11.146–47).

T'u Lung

Wan-Ming erh-shih-chia hsiao-p'in. "A Letter in Reply to Li Wei-yin" (47–48); "To a Friend, while Staying in the Capital" (48); "To a Friend, after Coming Home in Retirement" (48–49).

Wang Ssu-jen

Wang Chi-chung tsa-chu (Miscellaneous works of Wang Chi-chung). 2 vols. Reprint. Taipei: Wei-wen ch'u-pan-she, 1977. "Shan-hsi Brook" (II:653–54).
Wen-fan hsiao-p'in (Vignettes as literary meals). Edited by Chiang Chin-te. Ch'ang-sha: Yüeh-lu shu-she, 1989. "A Trip to Brimming Well" (3.243–44); "A Trip to Wisdom Hill and Tin Hill" (3.252–53); "Passing by the Small Ocean" (3.283–84).

Yüan Chung-tao

K'o-hsüeh-chai chi (Works from the Gemmy Snow Studio). Edited by Ch'ien Po-ch'eng. 3 vols. Shanghai: Shanghai ku-chi ch'u-pan-she, 1989. "Foreword to *The Sea of Misery*" (10.I:473–74); "Shady Terrace" (12.II:525); "Selections from *Wood Shavings of Daily Life*" (1:32.III:1111; 4:81.III:1196; 4:102.III:1200–1201; 5:39.III:1209; 6.III:1306).

Yüan Hung-tao

Yüan Hung-tao chi chien-chiao (Works of Yüan Hung-tao: A new edition with commentaries). Edited by Ch'ien Po-ch'eng. 2 vols. Shanghai: Shanghai ku-chi ch'u-pan-she, 1981. "First Trip to West Lake" (10.I:422); "Waiting for the Moon: An Evening Trip to the Six Bridges" (10.I:423–24); "A Trip to the Six Bridges after a Rain" (10.I:426); "Mirror Lake" (10.I:445); "A Trip to Brimming Well" (17.I:681); "A Trip to High Beam Bridge" (17.I:682–83); "A Biography of the Stupid but Efficient Ones" (19.I:723–25); "A Biography of Hsü Wen-ch'ang" (19.I:715–17).

Yüan Tsung-tao

Po-Su-tsai lei chi (Classified works from the Po-Su Studio). Edited by Ch'ien Po-ch'eng. Shanghai: Shanghai ku-chi ch'u-pan-she, 1989. "Little Western Paradise" (14.188–89); "A Trip to Sukhāvatī Temple" (14.192–93); "A Trip to Yüeh-yang" (14.194–95); "Miscellanea" (21.301–4).

Selected English-Language Works

The following list of works cited or consulted will be useful for readers who want to know more about traditional Chinese nonfictional belles-lettres prose, especially the *hsiao-p'in*, its authors, and more of their biographical, cultural, historical, and philosophical background.

Birch, Cyril, comp. and ed. *Anthology of Chinese Literature: From Early Times to the Fourteenth Century*. New York: Grove Press, 1965.

————, ed. *Anthology of Chinese Literature. Volume 2: From the Fourteenth Century to the Present Day*. New York: Grove Press, 1972.

————, ed. *Studies in Chinese Literary Genres*. Berkeley: University of California Press, 1974.

Bush, Susan, and Christian Murck, eds. *Theories of the Arts in China*. Princeton: Princeton University Press, 1983.

Chan, Albert. *The Glory and Fall of the Ming Dynasty*. Norman: University of Oklahoma Press, 1982.

Chan, Hok-lam, ed. *Li Chih (1527–1602) in Contemporary Chinese Historiography: New Light on His Life and Works*. New York: M. E. Sharpe, 1980.

Chan, Wing-tsit. *A Source Book in Chinese Philosophy*. Princeton: Princeton University Press, 1969.

Chang, Kang-i Sun. *The Late-Ming Poet Ch'en Tzu-lung: Crises of Love and Loyalism*. New Haven: Yale University Press, 1991.

Chaves, Jonathan. "The Expression of Self in the Kung-an School: Non-Romantic Individualism." In Hegel and Hessney, *Expressions of Self in Chinese Literature*.

————. "The Panoply of Images: A Reconsideration of Literary Theory of the Kung-an School." In Bush and Murck, eds., *Theories of the Arts in China*.

————. *Singing of the Source: Nature and God in the Poetry of the Chinese Painter Wu Li*. Honolulu: University of Hawaii Press, 1993.

————, trans. *Pilgrim of the Clouds: Poems and Essays by Yüan Hung-tao and His Brothers*. New York: Weatherhill, 1978.

Chen, Yu-shih. *Images and Ideas in Chinese Classical Prose: Studies of Four Masters*. Stanford: Stanford University Press, 1988.

Ch'en, Shou-yi. *Chinese Literature: A Historical Introduction*. New York: Ronald Press, 1961.

Chou, Chih-p'ing. *Yüan Hung-tao and the Kung-an School*. Cambridge: Cambridge University Press, 1988.

De Bary, William. Theodore, ed. *Self and Society in Ming Thought*. New York: Columbia University Press, 1970.

————, ed. *Sources of Chinese Tradition*. New York: Columbia University Press, 1960.

Dennerline, Jerry. *The Chia-ting Loyalists: Confucian Leadership and Social Change in Seventeenth-Century China*. New Haven: Yale University Press, 1981.

Egan. Ronald C. *The Literary Works of Ou-yang Hsiu (1007–72)*. Cambridge: Cambridge University Press, 1984.

————. *Word, Image, and Deed in the Life of Su Shih*. Cambridge: Cambridge University Press, 1994.

Goodrich, L. Carrington. *The Literary Inquisition of Ch'ien-lung*. Baltimore: Waverly Press, 1935.

———, and Chao-ying Fang, eds. *Dictionary of Ming Biography: 1368–1644*. 2 vols. New York: Columbia University Press, 1976.

Hargett, James M. *On the Road in Twelfth Century China: The Travel Diaries of Fan Chengda (1126–1193)*. Stuttgart: Franz Steiner Verlag Wiesbaden, 1989.

Hegel, Robert E. *The Novel in Seventeenth-Century China*. New York: Columbia University Press, 1981.

———, and Richard C. Hessney, eds. *Expression of Self in Chinese Literature*. New York: Columbia University Press, 1985.

Hsü Hsia-ko. Translated by Li Chi. *The Travel Diaries of Hsü Hsia-ko*. Hong Kong: Chinese University Press, 1974.

Huang, Ray. *A Year of No Significance: The Ming Dynasty in Decline*. New Haven: Yale University Press, 1981.

Hucker, Charles O., ed. *Chinese Government in Ming Times: Seven Studies*. New York: Columbia University Press, 1969.

———. *A Dictionary of Official Titles in Imperial China*. Stanford: Stanford University Press, 1985.

———. *The Traditional Chinese State in Ming Times: Seven Studies, 1368–1644*. Tucson: University of Arizona Press, 1961.

Hummel, Arthur W., ed. *Eminent Chinese of the Ch'ing Period: 1644–1912*. 2 vols. Washington, D.C.: U.S. Government Printing Office, 1943.

Hung Ming-shui. "Yüan Hung-tao and the Late Ming Literary and Intellectual Movement." Ph.D. diss., University of Wisconsin, 1974.

Jacobson, Roman, "The Dominant." In Ladislav Matejka and Krystyna Pomorska, eds., *Readings in Russian Poetics: Formalist and Structuralist Views*, pp. 82–90. Ann Arbor: University of Michigan Press, 1978.

Lai Ming. *A History of Chinese Literature*. New York: John Day, 1964.

Li, Chu-tsing, and James C. Y. Watt, eds. *The Chinese Scholar's Studio: Artistic Life in the Late Ming Period*. London: Thames and Hudson, 1987.

Lin, Yutang. *The Importance of Living*. New York: Reynal and Hitchcock, 1938.

———, trans. *Translations from the Chinese: The Importance of Understanding*. New York: World Publishing Company, 1960.

Liu I-ch'ing. Translated by Richard Mather. *Shih-shuo Hsin-yü: A New Account of Tales of the World*. Minneapolis: University of Minnesota Press, 1976.

Liu, James J. Y. *Essentials of Chinese Literary Art*. North Scituate, Mass.: Duxbury Press, 1979.

———. *Theories of Chinese Literature*. Chicago: Chicago University Press, 1975.

Liu Shih Shun, trans. *Chinese Classical Prose: The Eight Masters of the T'ang-Sung Period*. Hong Kong: Chinese University Press, 1979.

Lynn, Richard John. "Alternate Routes to Self-Realization in Ming Theories of Poetry." In Bush and Murck, eds., *Theories of the Arts in China*.

———. "Tradition and Synthesis: Wang Shih-chen as Poet and Critic." Ph.D. diss., Stanford University, 1961.

Mair, Victor H., ed. *The Columbia Anthology of Traditional Chinese Literature*. New York: Columbia University Press, 1995.

McCraw, David R. *Chinese Lyricists of the Seventeenth Century.* Honolulu: University of Hawaii Press, 1990.

Mote, Frederick W., and Denis Twitchett, eds. *The Cambridge History of China.* Vol. 7: *The Ming Dynasty, 1368–1644,* part 1. Cambridge: Cambridge University Press, 1988.

Nienhauser, William H., Jr., ed. and comp. *The Indiana Companion to Traditional Chinese Literature.* Bloomington: Indiana University Press, 1986.

———— et al. *Liu Tsung-yüan.* New York: Twayne, 1973.

Owen, Stephen, ed. and trans. *An Anthology of Chinese Literature: Beginnings to 1911.* New York: W. W. Norton, 1996.

————. *Readings in Chinese Literary Thought.* Cambridge, Mass.: Council on East Asian Studies, Harvard University, 1992.

————. *Remembrances: The Experience of the Past in Classical Chinese Literature.* Cambridge, Mass.: Harvard University Press, 1986.

Paper, Jordan D. *Guide to Chinese Prose.* 2nd ed. Boston: G. K. Hall, 1984.

Peterson, Willard. *Bitter Gourd: Fang I-chih and the Impetus for Intellectual Change.* New Haven: Yale University Press, 1979.

The Plum in the Golden Vase, or, Chin P'ing Mei. Translated by David T. Roy. Vol. 1, *The Gathering.* Princeton: Princeton University Press, 1993.

Poetry and Prose of the Ming and Qing. Peking: Panda Books, 1986.

Pollard, David E. *A Chinese Look at Literature: The Literary Values of Chou Tso-jen in Relation to the Tradition.* Berkeley: University of California Press, 1973.

Rickett, Adele A., ed. *Chinese Approaches to Literature from Confucius to Liang Ch'i-ch'ao.* Princeton: Princeton University Press, 1978.

Smith, Logan Pearsall. *All Trivia: A Collection of Reflections and Aphorisms.* Foreword by Gore Vidal. New York: Ticknor and Fields, 1984.

Spence, Jonathan D., and John E. Wills, Jr., eds. *From Ming to Ch'ing: Conquest, Region, and Continuity in Seventeenth-Century China.* New Haven: Yale University Press, 1979.

Strassberg, Richard E., trans. *Inscribed Landscapes: Travel Writing from Imperial China.* Berkeley: University of California Press, 1994.

Su Tung-P'o (Su Shih). Translated by Burton Watson. *Selected Poems by Su Tung-p'o.* Port Townsend, Wash.: Copper Canyon Press, 1994.

T'u Lung. Translated by Lin Yutang. *The Travels of Mingliaotse.* Shanghai: Hsi-feng She, 1940.

Wakeman, Frederic, Jr. *The Great Enterprise: The Manchu Reconstruction of Imperial Order in Seventeenth-Century China.* 2 vols. Berkeley: University of California Press, 1985.

————. "The Price of Autonomy: Intellectuals in Ming and Ch'ing Politics." *Daedalus* 101 (Spring 1972), pp. 35–70.

Woolf, Virginia. *Contemporary Writers.* London: Hogarth, 1965.

Wright, Arthur F., ed. *The Confucian Persuasion.* Stanford: Stanford University Press, 1960.

————. *Studies in Chinese Thought.* Chicago: Chicago University Press, 1953.

Wright, Arthur F., and Denis Twitchett, eds. *Confucian Personalities.* Stanford: Stanford University Press, 1962.

Wu, Pei-yi. *The Confucian's Progress: Autobiographical Writings in Traditional China.* Princeton: Princeton University Press, 1990.

Chinese Works

Ch'en Shao-t'ang. *Wan Ming hsiao-p'in lun-hsi* (An analysis of late Ming vignettes). Taipei: Yüan-liu ch'u-pan-she, 1982.

Ch'en Wan-i. *Wan-Ming hsiao-p'in yü Ming-chi wen-jen sheng-huo* (Vignettes of the late Ming and the life of the Ming literati). Taipei: Ta-an ch'u-pan-she, 1982.

Ch'en Wang-tao, ed. *Hsiao-p'in-wen ho man-hua* (New vignettes and cartoons). Shanghai: Sheng-huo shu-tien, 1935.

Cheng Chen-to. *Ch'a-t'u-pen Chung-kuo wen-hsüeh-shih* (Illustrated history of Chinese literature). 4 vols. Hong Kong: Shang-wu yin-shu-kuan, 1965.

Ch'ien Mu. "Chung-kuo wen-hsüeh chung te san-wen hsiao-p'in" (The prose vignettes in Chinese literature). In *Chung-kuo wen-hsüeh chiang-yen chi* (Collections of lectures on Chinese literature), pp. 50–64. Ch'eng-tu: Pa-Shu shu-she, 1987.

Hsia Hsien-ch'un, ed. *Ming liu-shih-chia hsiao-p'in wen ching p'in* (Best vignettes of sixty Ming authors). Shanghai: Shanghai she-hui k'o-hsüeh-yüan ch'u-pan-she, 1995.

———. *Ming-mo ch'i-ts'ai Chang Tai lun* (Genius of the closing years of the Ming: A study of Chang Tai). Shanghai: Shanghai she-hui k'o-hsüeh-yüan ch'u-pan-she, 1989.

Hu I-ch'eng, ed. *Ming Hsiao-p'in san-pai p'ien* (Three hundred Ming vignettes). Hsi-an: Hsi-pei ta-hsüeh ch'u-pan-she, 1992.

Huang K'ai-hua. "Wan-Ming k'o-chü yü shih-feng t'ui pai chih t'an-t'ao" (An investigation into the civil service examination and the degradation of the literati's morale in the late Ming). In his *Ming-shih lun-chi* (Essays on the history of the Ming), pp. 587–637. Kowloon: Ch'eng-ming ch'u-pan-she, 1972.

Jen Fang-ch'iu. *Yüan Chung-lang yen-chiu* (A study of Yüan Hung-tao). Shanghai: Shanghai ku-chi ch'u-pan-she, 1983.

Liang I-ch'eng. *Hsü Wei te wen-hsüeh yü i-shu* (The literary and art works of Hsü Wei). Taipei: I-wen ch'u-pan-she, 1976.

Liu I-ch'ing. Edited by Hsü Cheng-o. *Shih-shuo Hsin-yü chiao-chien* (An annotated edition of *A New Account of Tales of the World*). Hong Kong: Chung-hua shu-chü, 1987.

Liu Ta-chieh. *Chung-kuo wen-hsüeh fa-chan-shih* (A history of the development of Chinese literature). 3 vols. Shanghai: Shanghai ku-chi ch'u-pan-she, 1982.

Lu Jun-hsiang, ed. *Ming jen hsiao-p'in hsüan* (Selected vignettes of Ming authors). Ch'eng-tu: Ssu-ch'uan wen-yi ch'u-pan-she, 1986.

Lun-yü (Analects). In *Ssu shu wu ching* (The Four Books and the Five Classics). 3 vols. Tientsin: Ku-chi shu-tien, 1988.

Su Shih. *Tung-p'o chih-lin* (Tung-p'o's memorabilia). Edited by Wang Sung-ling. Peking: Chung-hua shu-chü, 1981.

————. *Tung-p'o chih-lin* / Ch'ou-ch'ih pi-chi (Tung-p'o's Memorabilia / Notes at Ch'ou-ch'ih). Edited by the Research Institute of Classics at East China Normal University. Shanghai: Hua-tung shih-fan ta-hsüeh ch'u-pan-she, 1983.

T'ang Kao-ts'ai, ed. *Li-tai hsiao-p'in ta-kuan* (A grand view of vignettes through the ages). Shanghai: San-lien shu-tien, 1991.

T'ien Su-lan. *Yüan Chung-lang wen-hsüeh yen-chiu* (A study of Yüan Hung-tao's literary works). Taipei: Wen-shih-che ch'u-pan-she, 1982.

Wang Shih-chen. *I-yüan chih-yen chiao chu* (An annotated edition of random remarks in the garden of art). Edited by Lo Chung-ting. Chi-nan: Ch'i Lu shu-she, 1992.

Yang Te-pen. *Yüan Chung-lang chih wen-hsüeh ssu-hsiang* (The literary thoughts of Yüan Hung-tao). Taipei: Wen-shih-che ch'u-pan-she, 1976.

Yüan Nai-ling. *Yüan Chung-lang yen-chiu* (A study of Yüan Hung-tao). Taipei: Hsüeh-hai ch'u-pan-she, 1981.

Index

Vignettes from the Late Ming
A *Hsiao-p'in* Anthology
Translated with Annotations and an Introduction by Yang Ye

This anthology presents seventy translated and annotated short essays, or *hsiao-p'in,* by fourteen well-known sixteenth- and seventeenth-century Chinese writers. *Hsiao-p'in,* characterized by spontaneity and brevity, were a relatively informal variation on the established classical prose style in which all scholars were trained. Written primarily to amuse and entertain the reader, *hsiao-p'in* reflect the rise of individualism in the late Ming period and collectively provide a panorama of the colorful life of the age. Critics condemned the genre as escapist because of its focus on life's sensual pleasures and triviality, and over the next two centuries many of these playful and often irreverent works were officially censored. Today, the essays provide valuable and rare accounts of the details of everyday life in Ming China as well as displays of wit and delightful turns of phrase.

"*Vignettes from the Late Ming* is a judicious selection of informal essays . . . [that] introduce aspects of traditional Chinese life that one cannot read about in more formal types of writing. These essays also tell us something about late-Ming sensibility and introduce the personality of some very interesting thinkers and writers. . . . A most welcome work."
—David R. Knechtges, University of Washington

"The selection is excellent; the best writers are included, and good examples by each. There is no [other] such anthology . . . available in any Western language."
—Jonathan Chaves, The George Washington University

Yang Ye is associate professor of comparative literature and foreign languages at the University of California, Riverside. He is the author of *Chinese Poetic Closure.*

Cover illustration: Li Liu-fang, *Landscape,* dated 1626. Museum of Far
Eastern Antiquities, The Swedish National Art Museums, Stockholm.
Cover design: Rebecca S. Neimark, Twenty-Six Letters

University of Washington Press   Seattle and London

ISBN 0-295-97733-7

90000

9 780295 977331